VITAL BO
Living with

Charlotte Bates

P

First published in Great Britain in 2019 by

Policy Press
University of Bristol
1-9 Old Park Hill
Bristol
BS2 8BB
UK
t: +44 (0)117 954 5940
pp-info@bristol.ac.uk
www.policypress.co.uk

North America office:
Policy Press
c/o The University of Chicago Press
1427 East 60th Street
Chicago, IL 60637, USA
t: +1 773 702 7700
f: +1 773-702-9756
sales@press.uchicago.edu
www.press.uchicago.edu

© Policy Press 2019

British Library Cataloguing in Publication Data
A catalogue record for this book is available from the British Library

Library of Congress Cataloging-in-Publication Data
A catalog record for this book has been requested

ISBN 978-1-4473-3506-1 paperback
ISBN 978-1-4473-3504-7 hardcover
ISBN 978-1-4473-3507-8 ePub
ISBN 978-1-4473-3508-5 Mobi
ISBN 978-1-4473-3505-4 epdf

Cover design by Emily Bates
Front cover image: Anna
Printed and bound in Great Britain by CMP, Poole
Policy Press uses environmentally responsible print partners

Contents

Illustrations   iv
Acknowledgements   v

Introduction   1
one   Eat   7
two   Exercise   21
three   Sleep   35
four   Genes and organs   45
five   Feet and legs   57
six   Hands and hearts   71
Conclusion   81

Appendix: Sensuous scholarship   93
Bibliography   107
Index   111

Illustrations

1. RIP pancreas by Alice
2. Walking stick by Anya
3. Aiden's journal
4. Aiden's journal
5. Ava's journal
6. Ava's journal
7. Alice's journal
8. Alice's journal
9. Anna's journal
10. Anna's journal
11. Anna's journal
12. Anna's journal
13. Anna's journal
14. Anna's journal
15. Polaroid of Ava's hands
16. Polaroid of Anya's legs
17. Injecting insulin (Alice: video diary)
18. Lucozade (Alice: video diary)
19. Bruised thigh (Alice: video diary)
20. Checking sugar level at night (Alice: video diary)
21. Tomato plant (Ami: video diary)
22. Cherry tomato (Ami: video diary)
23. Eye at night (Anna: video diary)
24. Jellyfish (Anna: video diary)
25. Snail (Anna: video diary)
26. Running shoes (Anna: video diary)
27. Drawing (Anna: video diary)
28. Feet (Anna: video diary)
29. Gardening gloves (Anna: video diary)
30. Carrots (Anna: video diary)
31. Running (Anna: video diary)
32. Lurching (Anna: video diary)
33. Post (Anya: video diary)
34. Stairs (Anya: video diary)
35. Sun salutations (Ava: video diary)
36. Slicing a lemon (Ava: video diary)
37. Coffee brewing (Ava: video diary)
38. Painting nails (Ava: video diary)
39. Comfy shoes (Ava: video diary)
40. High heels (Ava: video diary)

Acknowledgements

My first acknowledgement has to be to the twelve people who took part in this project – my heartfelt thanks to each of you for your time, candidness and trust. I hope that through this book they feel that their stories have contributed to something worthwhile. Everyone at Goldsmiths, where this study was made, has my deep thanks for their friendship over the years, especially Les Back, who has my deepest gratitude for his inspiration, generosity and guidance. I am grateful to Policy Press for taking on this project, and to my colleagues at Cardiff University, who have given me the time to write this book. I would also like to thank Emily Bates, who designed the cover for this book, and Anna, who photographed the tree. Lastly, my thanks go to my family for their patience and love.

Introduction

This book is the story of twelve people, each living with illness. Based on ethnographic research conducted over one year, it unfolds everyday experiences of living with a long-term physical or mental health condition, from asthma to bipolar disorder, depression, type 1 diabetes, epilepsy, joint hypermobility syndrome, muscular dystrophy and rheumatoid arthritis. In doing so, the book offers an innovative account of the body, health and illness in everyday life told from a sociological perspective. This account is not based on anguish, isolation and powerlessness but on the refusal to be crushed by illness, as Havi Carel (2008) writes, it is possible to find health, and happiness, within illness. Paying attention to the routine and unfolding aspects of embodied everyday life, the book aims to highlight the moments of care and repair through which people make their lives liveable. Learning from the lives portrayed, it explores ideas of care, vulnerability and choice, questioning what it means to live a modern life with illness and illuminating the vitality of bodies along the way.

In writing this book, I hope to bring into question what might be at stake in the care of ordinary bodies. Delving into the routines and rhythms of everyday life reveals the significance of the things that we usually take for granted, from what we eat to when we sleep, how we move and what we wear. Close attention to concealing strategies and rituals of care (a particular choice of clothing, the preparation of a meal) unfolds the relationship between the practical and ongoing achievement of living with illness, vulnerability and bodily doubt, and the felt politics of stigma in everyday life. Told from different perspectives, it shows how these mundane and seemingly simple aspects of living are complicated by illness, and made in/visible by the ways in which they are written on the body.

In doing so, the book shows how and why everyday life matters. To the participants in the study this is glaringly obvious; in illness, the body no longer lies beneath our everyday perception, and it is no longer possible to take it for granted. The certainty that our bodies will behave and that our time is our own dissipates. Instead of being absent, forgotten or quiet, the ill body is present, unforgettable and communicative. As Mariam Fraser and Monica Greco (2005: 20) write,

> We notice our body when the sudden or progressive impairment of one of its functions interferes with our daily activities, disturbing the order we take for granted. A leg

that will no longer walk, an eye that will no longer see, a heart that strains to run a familiar stretch, impose themselves on our attention as they transform our customary relation to the world.

In illness, mundane and ordinary acts become significant and remarkable, highlighting the raw and deep realities of our existence. The bleed between private and public spheres of life, the pretence of invisibility, the need for care and control, each reveal something of the daily reality of living with a chronic condition and act as reminders of our vulnerability and our mortality. It becomes important to ask what is at stake in our daily encounters.

While doctors, medical tests and hospital appointments all figure in these accounts, the book focuses primarily on the ways in which people learn to live with illness and take care of themselves, what Les Back (2015: 821) calls the 'ordinary triumphs of getting by'. This is because long-term illnesses often defy medicine. Unlike acute illnesses, which start suddenly and are quickly recovered from, or terminal illnesses, which loom with the certainty of death, long-term illnesses are neither transient nor final. They can be hard to diagnose and impossible to cure, they can flare up and retreat, but they never disappear completely. They are lived, throughout the life course. As such, it makes sense to study long-term conditions through the daily realities of self-management and self-care, and, like the participants in the study, to look to everyday life for answers. While medical accounts often treat these conditions individually, there are many commonalities across the spectrum of long-term illness, and the book also seeks to show the commonalities between different long-term conditions, bodies and lives.

These vital bodies are brought to the pages of this book with the help of the twelve people who took part in the study, in their spoken words and written thoughts, as well as drawings, photographs and video diaries. Bringing these gifts together, the book is an attempt to share experiences, insights and intimate moments, to recognise difficulties and to celebrate accomplishments. Each chapter combines thick descriptions, interview quotations, journal extracts and video diary footage in order to explore how individual lives are interconnected. These chapters are a form of portraiture, an account of life as it unfolds, and a way of evoking intimacy. At night, in rituals of care, and in memories and reflections, they offer a series of intimate encounters with the sensuous, the tangible and the intangible sensation of living with illness. These stories are collected as examples, not evidence. They are examples that are attentive to the unruly details of ill bodies and the difficulties of everyday life, and they are drawn together in order to make connections and evoke experiences that others might relate to. As such, these accounts are written and illustrated in ways that I hope will make them open, recognisable and legible both to the people whose lives they are based on and to a broad readership. These partial accounts are offered as a series of fragments, and the aim is not to indicate unfortunate gaps but rather to present an imperfect account (Clifford, 1986: 8). These accounts are also translations, and like any translation they are at risk of falling flat or missing the right note. As John Ciardi (2013: ix) writes of the act of translating between languages:

> When the violin repeats what the piano has just played, it cannot make the same sounds and it can only approximate the same chords. It can, however, make recognisably the same 'music', the same air. But it can only do so when it is as faithful to the self-logic of the violin as it is to the self-logic of the piano.

This book, then, is concerned with listening, in two different ways. Sociology is a listener's art (Back, 2007), and the ways in which I learned to listen to these accounts and bring them to attention are outlined in the methodological appendix. But listening to the body is also something that all of the participants are attentive to, in their own ways, and the book is concerned with the ways in which they have learned to listen to the ill body as it murmurs, shouts and screams for what it needs or wants. In both living lives with illness and in taking part in this study, the participants became observers, or listeners, and it is through their accounts that we come to know their day-to-day worlds. In an attempt not to mistranslate their experiences, the book moves between the participants' words and my own, drawing on their voices while offering contextual support and sociological interpretation. In a study of repeated acts of stethoscopic listening to heart sounds or 'murmurs', Tom Rice (2008) shows how repeated medical practices of listening can reify and isolate aspects of the body, turning them into objectified clinical cases. His example provides a useful counterpoint to the listening practices in this book, which are more subjective and familiar.

One of the aims of writing this book has been to portray personal accounts, and to make illness less anonymous. But all of the names in this book are fictitious – each one begins with the letter 'A' to remind the reader of this anonymity. As Tom Hall (2017: 19) writes, 'who sees who and on what terms, who sees their (own) name in print – has to be managed'. Pseudonyms are used to protect individual identities and to afford some privacy, while making lives visible.

The first three chapters take inspiration from one of the participants' mantras. 'Fish, exercise, sleep' is a phrase that Ava repeats in her head and sometimes writes down; it is a code for living which helps her recalibrate so that everything else can fall into place. The first chapter, 'Eat', focuses on the importance of diet, showing how the basic need to eat can become a defining feature of our lives, whether we are calculating carbohydrates, seeking the nutrition that our bodies need, or controlling their shape and size. Through eating, the processes and practices that create routines, rules, cures and rituals of care become visible, and the ways in which the body is reconfigured by its material needs become apparent. As a significant form of managing illness, eating is a way of caring for the body, but it is one that creates conflict, turning eating into a duty and a reward. Ava has rheumatoid arthritis. In her search for a magic bullet to cure her of her daily aches and pains, she has consulted nutritionists, bought supplements, subscribed to diet and nutrition email lists, and read countless magazines, books and websites. Disciplined eating forms part of Ava's strategy for health, and routines structured around food provide a sense of security and control, revealing significant dedication to caring for the body.

The second chapter, 'Exercise', considers the rhythm of our bodies in motion and the complicated relationships between exercise and illness, as both a necessity and a joy. Like eating, the significance of exercise is redefined by illness, and the body is maintained, challenged and re-known through it. Exercise regimes can provide control, treatment and an alternative form of medication so that through physical activity bodies feel strong, independent and free in spite of illness. But ill bodies are prone to overexertion, and exercise can reinforce their dependence and vulnerability as well as their strength. For Anna, who has depression, exercise has become a form of self-medication. Running and cycling regularly make her feel less depressed, so she tries to be physically active at least four times a week. Disruption to this routine can cause her mood to plummet quickly, showing the dependence that she has on her body.

The third chapter, 'Sleep', looks at how the demands of our working and social lives can conflict with the demands of our body, and at how illness redefines our lives through the need to sleep. While rest is sometimes the best cure for illness, sleep clashes with social expectations, destroys routines and causes conflicts. The need to sleep is perhaps the most delicate revelation of the body's vulnerability, and bodies that need more sleep simply do not fit in with the demands of modern life.

As such, they present themselves as things that demand care, that are frail and difficult to manage. Aiden has rheumatoid arthritis and rest is a better cure than any drug, but with a modern life in London it is the hardest thing to come by. Sometimes his body screams for sleep, to rest and rejuvenate, evidencing the conflict between how Aiden wants to live and what his body needs.

The fourth chapter, 'Genes and organs' examines how the interiors of our bodies structure and influence our exterior surfaces and identities and shape our daily lives, and how the inner workings of our bodies, the circulations of blood and the flows of air, affect and betray us. This chapter traces the transmission of conditions from their interior origins within the body to the outside world of everyday life and considers how the inner landscapes of the body are both visible and significant. Ami has asthma. She has learned the warning signals of an asthma attack, from the wheezing sound originating from her chest, to the tight feeling in her shoulders, and the sudden pain in her teeth. She knows when to take her inhaler, and she also knows when to reach for the phone and call the emergency services. In moments like these, illness is transported from the safe and invisible interior of the body to the outside world.

Moving from the interior to the exterior, the book continues with the fifth chapter, 'Feet and legs', body parts that, as our connection to the earth and our way of navigating through the world, are perhaps our most direct link to the landscapes in which we live. How do our feet and legs, as well as the shoes and canes that accompany them, connect us to, negotiate us through, and redefine how we know the built environment? How do our bodies redefine the topography of our worlds? This chapter considers the importance of these seemingly simple body parts and the influence that they have on the ways in which we move, dress and travel. Anya has muscular dystrophy and the muscles in her legs are wasting away. But by finding new ways of using her body, and by learning her environment in detail, she has held onto her ability to walk and her independence.

The sixth chapter, 'Hands and hearts', considers the emotional connections between bodies, minds and landscapes, and touches on themes of finding a home and belonging in the world. Through this chapter, we see how bodies find their own routes through the spaces of everyday life, and how, just as illness refuses to be contained within bodies, bodies refuse to be confined by illness. Anna, who has depression, does not have any of the same doubts about her hands as she does about her mind and its thoughts. She never thinks twice about their ability to do things, and they do not seem to suffer from the same anxiety and self-hatred that she does. Anna's acute mind-body split illustrates how she belongs in the world through her body and at the same time feels distant from it.

Up to a point, the book is based on 'snapshots'. These 'images taken (out) of passing life' (Hall, 2017: 7) were all collected together over one year, and while some of the methods that were used drew out longer life histories and trajectories, the interviews, journals, images and video diaries could only ever hope to provide a momentary glimpse into the lived realities of living with illness. But, in the summer of 2016, seven years after the original study was conducted, I contacted the participants again. I had not set out to conduct longitudinal research, but the process of writing this book threw up an unexpected opportunity to return to their lives and ask how they were living now, what had changed, and what had remained the same. Just as cultures (Clifford, 1986: 10) and cities (Back and Keith, 2014: 25) do not hold still for their portraits, neither do people, and as I found out, many of the participants had moved on or away, meaning it was not always possible to meet in person. Nor had their illnesses held still, as we will see.

Despite the passage of time, eight of the twelve participants responded to my invitation to meet again, and follow-up interviews were conducted in various locations across London, in other cities, and, when it was not possible to meet in person, by online conversations. Recalling the *Up* documentary series produced by Granada Television, which has followed the lives of fourteen British children every seven years since 1964, when they were seven years old, each chapter begins with findings from the original study and ends with insights from the follow-up study, enfolding and unfolding embodied life as it is lived through time. The passage of seven years makes the relationship between life, illness and time apparent, illuminating the ups and downs of everyday life, and the ebbs and flows of illness.

The book ends with two more academic chapters, in the form of a conclusion and a methodological appendix. Learning from the lives portrayed, the conclusion seeks to relate some of these findings to other literatures and ways of thinking about illness in more detail, providing some evidence for the arguments that the book makes and offering a more theoretical discussion. The appendix provides more detail about how the study was conducted, and offers some craft lessons in visual sociology and sensuous scholarship, told through illustrative fieldwork tales.

ONE

Eat

'Eat' focuses on the importance of diet, showing how the basic need to eat can become a defining feature of our lives, whether we are calculating carbohydrates, seeking the nutrition that our bodies need, or controlling their shape and size. Eating highlights the potential conflicts that illness can produce, conflicts between what a body wants to eat and what it needs to eat, in the demands that it places on how we buy and prepare food, and in when and where it can be eaten. Through eating, the processes and practices that create routines, rules and rituals of care become visible, showing that eating is both a duty and a reward, a way of controlling illness and a way of caring for the body.

One relationship to eating defines food as a way of controlling illness and caring for the body. To make this relationship, individuals must be disciplined in their approach to diet. Long lists of foods to eat and foods to avoid are formulated in order to minimise the impact of illness and increase a feeling of good health. Lists of foods are developed in response to instruction and advice, from personal research, and by listening to the body itself. While there may be evidence for many of these measures, and while they often make a difference, the underlying promise of disciplined eating is the feeling of control that it creates. Sometimes food is the main, even the only, means available of controlling a condition that defies medical treatment, promising power over an illness that is otherwise uncontrollable. As Ava writes in her journal:

> Sometimes I think of going back to a nutritionist but I realise I am probably looking for something that no one can provide and that is a magic bullet, or more simply, a list of instructions which if I carefully adhered to would make me 100% not swollen and would guarantee that I'd have full function of my hands and feet for the rest of my life. (Ava: journal)

Ava is thirty-two and has rheumatoid arthritis. Just as there is no known cause of rheumatoid arthritis there is also no known cure, and the course of the condition is impossible to predict. In her search for a magic bullet, Ava has consulted nutritionists, bought and taken supplements, subscribed to diet and nutrition email lists, and read countless magazines, books and websites. Information continuously flows towards her body, demanding an investment of time and money but allowing her to stay active in her approach to living with illness. Because it is an inflammatory disease, rheumatoid arthritis can affect the heart and other internal organs, so, for example, people with rheumatoid arthritis have a higher incidence of heart attacks and heart disease. For this reason, Ava has read books about inflammation in the body and has discovered that certain foods can exacerbate inflammation, and that foods containing Omega 3 and 6, like fish, are good to eat. The list of things she 'should' do daily includes drinking eight glasses of water, eating five servings of fruit and veg, taking a B12 supplement, and getting Omega 3s by eating nuts, seeds or oily fish (but not more than two servings per week). Things she should avoid, or at least not overindulge in, include: caffeine, sugar, alcohol, red meat, dairy, citrus fruits and vegetables in the nightshade family (eggplant, potatoes and tomatoes), and saturated fat. A video tour of her kitchen cupboards reveals no fewer than ten types of tea, most of which owe their place in the cupboard to the health benefits that they offer. There is green tea, which has many health benefits; white tea, which is slightly less caffeinated than green and supposedly better; peppermint tea for digestion; pleasure tea that does not have caffeine and just tastes nice; fair trade tea bags for visitors looking for builder's tea; chamomile, a good detox; liquorice tea in the back; tea from Rwanda and Sri Lanka; and another tea containing cinnamon, cardamom and ginger, all supposedly good for inflammation.

The items on Ava's list are well researched and specifically selected for their capacity to control inflammation in the body, but they are also controversial and sometimes contradictory. A conversation with her doctor, for example, can quickly undermine the power she ascribes to her diet:

> 'I try not to eat that much dairy, and I really like eating cheese, so sometimes if I eat lots of cheese it makes me feel more swollen, so I'll start telling him this, and he'll just be like, there is no evidence that shows that what you eat affects your rheumatoid arthritis. And even though there might not be I believe it, I believe it's true, it's true for me.'
> (Ava: interview)

The hard line being drawn here between medical knowledge and personal truth only serves to make the search for answers harder.

Because there is no certainty, keeping up a disciplined approach to eating can be difficult:

> I suppose it's much easier to make sacrifices when you are promised - or guaranteed - results. But when you are making sacrifices + you still feel swollen in your hands, you wonder why you are bothering… (Ava: journal)

Social situations often demand the consumption of foods that are on the list of items to be avoided, and visits with family and friends can easily lead to the rules being ignored. The consequences are manifested in swollen and sensitive joints, so that simple pleasures have become indulgences, and not caring for or paying attention to her body has an acutely felt price. While Ava loves food and loves to cook, arthritis has transformed eating into a balancing act in which she thinks about food primarily in terms of what it gives her. It is a matter of constantly monitoring how swollen she feels and knowing when to be more careful without taking it too far – during the times when she has been more extreme about diet her friends have told her she is too thin. Now, she picks and chooses the indulgences to allow herself: '…it's just too boring of a life to avoid sugar, coffee and alcohol every day, so I try to pick one or two and just indulge moderately' (Ava: video diary).

Through her love of food, Ava has made up for the instances when she feels deprived by the foods she should not eat by creating food rituals that give her pleasure. One of Ava's rituals is a weekly walk to Greenwich through the foot tunnel to buy a loaf of rye bread at the bakery there. A nutritionist once told her to avoid eating wheat, and, while she was frustrated by the idea of adding another item to her list of things to avoid, and still is not completely convinced that it is a necessary measure, she does try to eat rye bread instead of wheat bread. She enjoys the morning walk and coming home with a beautiful rye loaf makes her feel less deprived, which is really, really important.

In her video diary, Ava records the movements, textures and aromas of her morning routine. The routine includes preparing a glass of water with freshly squeezed lemon, a drink that forms part of the complex relationship that she has with her rheumatoid arthritis. In the opening shot Ava's bed lies empty, still crumpled and warm from her body. There is a momentary pause before thumb and forefinger turn and twist a plastic handle, opening the metal blind to let the early morning light in. The streetlights, still illuminated, shine palely through the dark blue sky and down onto the residential street. Toes flex, feeling for the support of the yoga mat before the video camera swings up and away, turning the room and its contents upside down then swinging slowly back to her toes, fuzzy at first, but with just enough time to come into focus before the video camera swings away again, passing a shadow on the carpet, returning to the mat in a smoothly flowing arc. A healthy body glows from the front of a shiny magazine cover at the top of a pile of titles that have been consulted in the search for a healthy lifestyle. Water pours from a clear jug and air bubbles rise to the top of the glass as it fills. Her hands grasp a lemon and a knife, working the blade swiftly back and forth in an action that slices the fruit in half. She squeezes one half into the glass, fingers working to release drops of juice that cloud the water. A wall clock indicates that it is 6:33 am; seconds tick by. She reaches to pick up the glass, lifting it out of shot. The video camera remains fixed on the kitchen worktop; green and yellow apples fill a basket. The sound of the water being gulped, swallowed, drunk seems to fill the screen before the almost emptied glass is returned to the worktop and the video camera switch is clicked off.

Ava's narrative runs over this sequence, as she explains how sleep, exercise and diet are interconnected and crucial to the everyday management of her condition:

> I usually like to start my day with some kind of physical activity, but that only happens if I get enough sleep. At the very least, I can do some sun salutations. I used to do a yoga DVD, but somehow it got to the bottom of the pile. I spend a lot of money looking for answers, even though I know better. One book told me, every morning I should have room temperature water, with the juice of a fresh lemon, finished off with a pinch of cayenne pepper (which I don't have). I should drink all this before anything else. This morning routine means I can't just roll out of bed and leave the house, and normally it keeps me busy an hour before I leave. (Ava: video diary)

Another ritual transforms making coffee, which strictly speaking she should not drink, into a special act of care. Recorded on video, the sounds of coffee brewing – the electric buzz of the machine, the gurgling water and the drip of the coffee pot slowly filling up – evoke the smell of freshly brewed coffee filling the room and bring the intimacy of the ritual to the screen. The camera is fixed on the coffee maker with its orange on light glowing warmly, and as the minutes pass the black coffee froths and rises inside the glass jug while an empty mug waits expectantly beside it. With Ava, I am patiently waiting for the coffee to finish brewing, and, as I wait, I begin to understand the significance of this seemingly ordinary start to the day, which connects Ava to childhood memories, and through the small acts of others makes her feel cared for:

> I love coffee; I love its flavour, its warmth, it's very comforting to me. There's something about the sound of a coffee maker, it just makes you feel like your day is off to a really good start! When I do research about diet and arthritis, coffee is one thing that you're really supposed to avoid. But I feel so deprived without a cup a day, and sometimes I have two. Sometimes I have thought that making coffee is a meaningless ritual, and that I could just substitute it with something else. Instead of turning on the coffee maker I could make a cup of tea. But tea doesn't have the same texture to me, or the taste. The funny thing is, I don't know how to work this coffee machine, and my housemate sets it up the night before. And maybe that's a bit of what it's about, somebody looking after me in a way. My grandmother always had a coffee pot set to automatic; she didn't even have to hit the switch, it was just ready when she woke up. Making a cup of coffee this way takes so much longer than a cup of tea, you really have to be patient. (Ava: video diary)

Anya has Miyoshi-type muscular dystrophy, a form of distal myopathy. It is a genetic condition, and both parents must be carrying the gene in order to pass it on. Miyoshi's belongs to a group of muscular dystrophies called dysferlinopathies; the body fails to produce a protein called dysferlin, and this causes muscle deterioration. Miyoshi's is extremely rare and little is known about it, but it is known that the condition isolates itself to the distal muscles – the muscles furthest away from the centre of the body – and that it manifests itself differently in different people's bodies. At the age of thirty-one, Anya has now lost most of the muscles in both her legs: her gastrocnemius, the anterior of her lower legs and her quadriceps, and the condition is starting to take out her pectorals and the muscles in her arms. It is a rare condition with no known treatment, and no one can really provide the answers that Anya needs. As a result, Anya has had to work it out for herself. Like Ava, one of the ways in which she tries to stay healthy is by paying attention to diet:

'I guess the other part is diet, that's also your body saying I need to eat this; I need to not touch this. And I always think, you know, I never know how much real logic there is to that, sometimes you could be saying I shouldn't eat this or I should eat this, and it might not actually have an effect at all, but it gives you a sense that you've got some kind of control.' (Anya: interview)

Although it is hard to be sure of the value of food, Anya's approach to diet originates from her body's needs. She listens to what it wants and to what it doesn't, and tries to respond to those requests. So, for example, she avoids processed foods, stays away from things containing wheat and gluten, eats lots of yeast, tries to have lots of good oils and fats and avoid the bad ones, eats lots of vegetables and not much meat, and avoids caffeine and alcohol. These measures help her digestion and provide valuable energy, so that her body is able to focus on all the other things it needs to do. This eating regime is not only about what works, it is also about maintaining a sense of control. The effort required to maintain a disciplined approach to eating puts Anya in touch with her body and makes her active against her condition, transforming food into an essential and positive aspect of her life, so that through eating she is able to reclaim her body from the grip of illness.

Anna is forty-three and has been living with depression since her childhood. Like Ava and Anya, her diet is strictly controlled, something other people might perceive as a form of extremism. She doesn't drink or smoke, and she is virtually vegetarian. Diet is one of the ways in which she is able to construct a routine and feel healthy through her body:

'It works for me. It feels like I've found a way to feel better. I imagine that if I stopped it wouldn't be very good. I was ill over Christmas with flu, and I felt a real plunge. But as soon as I started to re-do the things I do I felt fine.' (Anna: interview)

Alec, is thirty-four and has bipolar disorder. Also known as manic-depressive illness, bipolar disorder is a mood disorder characterised by rapid or significant changes in mood, specifically between a manic, elevated mood with associated behaviours, and a low, depressive mood. For the last two years Alec has been managing his condition without taking medication. He has put certain things that he can rely on in place, like diet, so that he now feels self-sufficient and able to take care of himself. The extent to which Alec is following his beliefs about eating is a good indicator of his health. His ability to maintain his diet, which for six years was strictly vegetarian, and his grip on other demands in his life and his mood are interrelated and dependent on one another, evidencing the far reaches of control that can be gained, and lost, through the eating body:

> 'I think a lot about it [diet], I have lots of beliefs about it – that I don't always follow because, again, like, if the mood gets away from you then other things crumble, but then if those things crumble that will exacerbate the mood.' (Alec: interview)

For Ava, Anya, Anna and Alec, disciplined eating forms part of a strategy for health. Routines structured around food reveal significant dedication to caring for the body, provide a sense of security and control, and unite mind and body in an attempt to manage illness. But maintaining these regimes requires energy, motivation and work, all of which can be hard to find.

When disciplined eating fails, another relationship to eating is constructed. This relationship is characterised by feeling unable to cope with the body and its needs. As a result, mind and body are distanced from each other, leading to feelings of guilt towards the body. Amelia is twenty-four and has been living with depression for the last four years. The tiredness, anxiety and lack of motivation symptomatic of being depressed affect her ability to look after herself and make healthy eating difficult. During her first serious attack, she visited a psychiatrist who advised her to stop drinking alcohol and to get her diet under control. But even though she really wanted to try to do this, Amelia didn't feel at that moment as though she had the agency and the willpower to be able to take control of her life. Instead she binged on comfort food, not having the energy or the drive to go grocery shopping or to cook. Just walking to the shops had become too stressful and exhausting. This, combined with medication, which had increased her appetite, meant that by her twenty-first birthday Amelia had put on a significant amount of weight, leaving her feeling horrible and heavy. She had no sex drive and she hated being touched. Her body felt different. Not that it had become alien to her, but rather that she had become trapped in it. It seems obvious to think that people who have depression are trapped in their minds, and the feeling was like that, but it was not just that; Amelia had also become trapped in her body. It was a sensation of being blocked, of feeling like a stone. The interdependence of eating and depression continue to affect Amelia's life, and her depression is not located, but felt, in her stomach, which is the register of the bad effects of her condition:

> '…when I feel bad and I feel like I'm not healthy enough to do things like go outside and achieve things and stuff like that, it's often because I haven't eaten enough, or I've eaten too much, or I've eaten the wrong thing, and it's combined with feeling bad and having not slept and stuff, so a lot of the time I feel quite shaky or empty when I'm going through these periods.' (Amelia: interview)

Similarly, April recognises the snowball effect that connects the frequency of her epileptic seizures to her alcohol consumption and diet. Over the last few years she has begun to improve her lifestyle – eating healthily, avoiding alcohol, and sleeping regularly – in order to reduce the number of seizures that she has. But April finds it hard to maintain a healthy lifestyle, and at the age of twenty-eight she still goes out drinking when she shouldn't, ruining the hard work that she has put in. As a consequence, she worries that she doesn't look after her body, and it leaves her feeling disappointed. Her frustration shows that illness transforms eating from a taken-for-granted activity into an act with significant physical and emotional repercussions: 'I feel disappointed, slightly angry, because I'm a bit cross with myself for letting it happen, because it can be controlled' (April: interview).

For others food seems less significant. Ami and Aiden both choose not to pay too much attention to the dietary recommendations associated with their conditions, instead eating the things that they like:

> 'I shouldn't have milk, but I'm a dairy fiend. I'm not allergic to milk, but I've been told that milk is not good for asthmatics, because of the mucous and everything, the traces that are left behind, but I can't help it, I love milk.' (Ami: interview)

> 'I take supplements, cod liver oil, and I eat a lot of fish, stuff like that. But I'm a bit of a hypocrite in that way, in that I shouldn't eat tomato and I shouldn't eat eggplant … I decide on how convenient and tasty it is - like not eating tomato, are you kidding? You try doing that, I like tomato and it's a base for so many things, like if I just want a quick pasta … But I don't notice that much of a difference with

it anyway … I don't know, I'm not saying it doesn't work, but if I skip tomato for two days then of course I'm not going to feel any difference.' (Aiden: interview)

In these instances, diet is less central. But eating is not simply about prohibition: as Ami and Aiden show, illness forces us to consider all of the ways in which diet might help or hinder our bodies. The fact that a glass of milk or a tomato sauce could be a serious threat to the body heightens our awareness of all that we are privileged to.

For Adam, who is twenty-three and has been living with type 1 diabetes since he was eighteen, ignoring the needs of his body in relation to eating is a more definite risk. Adam has to check his sugar levels on a regular basis: when he wakes up in the morning, before he eats, a couple of hours after he eats, and before he goes to bed. Every time he eats he takes an insulin injection, and once every twenty-four hours he takes a base insulin injection. If he keeps to this routine he feels fine, but every now and then he will lose his pens, or forget an injection, or just not be disciplined enough, and then he can feel the sugar building up, the stiffness setting in, and he will get ratty and snap at people. While Adam knows that eating healthily is an important part of living with diabetes, he describes his attitude to diet as 'a bit lazy':

'But when I eat, yeah, cutting out all the sugary drinks, the full sugar cokes and everything like that, that was alright, I wasn't too bad about that, but it's the sweets – I've got a really bad sweet tooth, chocolate, and sticky toffee puddings and donuts, they're the hard ones, they're the devil! But in those cases, I should take a little shot of insulin, it's there for me to do it, but I'm just a bit lazy, that's all.' (Adam: interview)

His attitude toward eating has led to arguments with his girlfriend. Adam thinks that while he is young he should just enjoy himself. His girlfriend thinks that if he does not look after himself now he will not be able to enjoy himself later on in life. Adam knows she is right, that if he does not take care there could be complications - that diabetes can lead to loss of limbs, blindness or kidney disease - but for now he is trying not to think about that. Perhaps when he is a bit older, in a couple of years, he will take it more seriously, but right now he just wants to have fun. Having to eat when he does not necessarily want to, needing to be disciplined about eating and to keep to a routine all conflict with Adam's outlook, changing the meaning of food, demanding that his body act against its own desires and constantly reminding him of the presence of illness. His attitude to eating represents a third relationship, in which the body's needs are ignored and its vulnerability denied.

To different degrees, eating is significant for everyone. Food forms part of a search for answers and can be a source of control, offering the possibility of becoming healthier in response to illness. The control that food seems to offer through the certainty of cause and effect is reassuring, but it is also tainted. As Ava explained, it is a sense of control that is not necessarily true – but even knowing that she cannot control her arthritis is somehow control, in a way. What is important is that she knows her condition, that it is familiar and that she understands it, and diet is one way of making that relationship. Establishing and recognising cause and effect – whether through food, exercise or sleep – makes the body feel more stable, as Aiden writes in his journal:

> I don't know why I blame things for my A. getting aggravated at times, I know sometimes that it just gets bad for no reason at all, or that sometimes it's fine when there are so many reasons why it shouldn't be. A lot of the time the A. will follow a loose cause and effect pattern but not always, but I prefer it when it does – not just simply a case of my body being faulty with me having no control over it. (Aiden: journal)

But diet can also be misleading. In his thirteen-year search for a diagnosis to explain his pain, food allergy was one of the many dead ends that Adrian pursued. And when food is made important, it inevitably entails the possibility that the body will become a source of guilt. The demands of disciplined eating make the body dependent, regimented and inflexible, and the heightened awareness of what should and should not be consumed is only intensified by the potential list of things that might happen if good control is not kept.

For Alice, who is twenty-five and has type 1 diabetes, this list includes blindness, kidney failure, stroke, heart attack, gangrene, numbness (in feet and hands), producing sick children, not producing children at all, depression and loss of sex drive. Type 1 diabetes typically strikes in adolescence, and unlike type 2 diabetes it is unpreventable. In type 1, which accounts for about 10% of all diabetics, the pancreas stops producing insulin, which means that the body can't break down any sort of carbohydrate or glucose. If untreated, this will trigger a famine reaction in the body, and it will begin eating itself, starting with its fatty reserves.

Having diabetes involved the imposition of an inconvenient regime on Alice's teenage life, including an injection at 7 o'clock in the morning – fine on a school day but not so convenient on weekends – and dinner by 7 o'clock in the evening, which didn't fit in with the family routine. But with the support of her family helping her to cope, she imagined that her new regime would be a really good way to be healthy. It wasn't until she left home for university that life with diabetes started to get really difficult; the problem with diabetes, she told me, is that the minute you change your regime in any way your body reacts; the slightest change in your life, the slightest stress, will affect it. At home, she had felt pretty confident and relaxed, but university life, with its pressures and alcohol driven social scene, threw her, and it threw the diabetes. Alice began to feel insecure, and felt that she was failing. Even today, after ten years of coping with diabetes on a daily basis, Alice feels like she is constantly failing her body exam.

The regime she is on now, called DAFNE (Dose Adjustment For Normal Eating), involves having to inject five times a day; two long-term-acting insulin injections, one in the morning and one at night, and one regular insulin injection for each meal she has. DAFNE is designed to enable greater flexibility with eating, but it means that Alice has to be aware of how much carbohydrate is in everything. She has to weigh everything out, perhaps check her book, which lists how much carbohydrate is in most things, and work out the ratio of insulin to carbohydrate, which can vary depending on her sugar levels. This means that she has numbers in her head all the time and she is constantly trying to do mathematics. Breakfast is quite easy, because she's normally at home and she knows how much carbohydrate is in a banana, and how much is in a small bowl of muesli with milk. But the problems start around lunchtime, when she is out. A sandwich is ok, and if she's having a salad then she doesn't need to inject, because there is no carbohydrate in that. But a hot chocolate would be more complicated to work out, and not everything can be found in the book. Even if she gets the mathematics right, there are a host of other things that can throw Alice's diabetes off balance, and a drop in her sugar levels can trigger a 'hypo' – a hypoglycaemic episode. Everything has to be factored into a strict regime, and even then there are no guarantees. Her list of things she is meant to do includes:

> Write down my sugar levels
> Write down what I eat and its carb count
> Weigh my food

Check sugars only at meals, exercise, bed, or when feeling
a hypo
Inject for every carb portion I eat over 1 (breakfast,
lunch, dinner, snacks). (Alice: journal)

For Alice, the consumption of food is legislated by more than a list
of instructions. What she eats is continuously redefined in response
to her condition. The need to constantly monitor her body and be
reactive to it, to eat or drink what and when she doesn't want to, turns
food from a source of nourishment into a form of medication that
often contradicts the attempts she makes to control her weight and
be otherwise healthy:

> 'It's quite frustrating in that sense. Especially if you're
> exercising to lose weight, it's very frustrating to need some
> Lucozade after, or eat something; it kind of misses the
> point really. Yesterday I was trying to be very good … but
> I hypo-ed three times in the day and it led to having to eat
> a load of crap.' (Alice: interview)

Conducting a *Spendaholics* or *You Are What You Eat* reality show-
style shock tactic for herself, Alice decided to record a tidy up of her
bedroom on video. She found twenty-two empty Lucozade bottles
in her room and lined them up along the foot of her bed; six weeks'
worth of bottles, not including her glucose tables or the bottles she
had left at her boyfriend's or drank while she was out. Lucozade has a
high glucose content and can be rapidly absorbed by the body, so when
Alice's sugar levels are low it is the perfect thing to reach for in order
to prevent a hypo. The display quantified the presence of Lucozade in
Alice's body and her life, and amounted to a worrying, but necessary,
consumption of sugar and unhealthy chemicals.

Finally, eating can also be self-destructive. Sometimes Alice finds
herself eating when she really should not, as she revealed in her video
diary:

> Yesterday I found myself in my flat, I was meant to be
> working and just couldn't, and the way to fill that void is
> through noshing. I ate two carrots, two bits of celery, two
> yoghurts, I made myself a banana cake and ate two slices
> of that, my flatmate treated us to some chocolates, and
> this doesn't include my meals. So, I was constantly eating,
> constantly telling myself I don't care, I don't care! And

obviously by about midnight I was realising that wasn't a
good idea... (Alice: video diary)

In listening to the body, the significance of the basic need to eat
becomes clear. No longer a basic bodily drive that can be taken for
granted, eating reveals the centrality of the body in our attempts to live
with illness. Paying attention to what, why and when we eat shows
how eating and illness are entangled, and made present by everyday acts
and in everyday places. Sometimes they reinforce the negative presence
of illness, but they can also help to make positive connections to the
body. As a significant form of managing illness, eating is a way of caring
for the body, but it is one that creates conflict, turning eating into a
duty and a reward. The making and breaking of routines is intimately
linked to our ability to look after our bodies, both connecting us to
them and distancing us from them. Ultimately, eating begins to reveal
a picture of illness in which, instead of trying to silence our bodies,
we learn to listen to them.

★★★

Seven years have passed, and Ava is six weeks away from turning forty.
She is in a relationship, and has moved to a new city to live with her
partner. Her rheumatoid arthritis has settled down, to the point where
she was dismissed from regular appointments at her rheumatology
clinic. She is now medication-free, but her awareness of the need to
care for her body remains acute, and she still places great importance
on diet to keep her body healthy:

> 'I am conscious though that I do feel that if I am not
> careful in terms of looking after myself that I could start
> feeling sick again, so I am trying to keep a healthy balance
> in my life, which is so hard ... For me it's been a whole
> journey of self-care really, and I rarely get sick now.'
> (Ava: follow-up interview)

It has been difficult to explain this need for self-care to her partner,
who has only known her in this period of good health. To him, the
arthritis seems abstract, not a part of everyday life. She will refer to it

when she wants to make a point, explaining that she was unwell and she does not want to be unwell again; that she wants to do as much as she can to stay healthy; and she has to be quite firm about her diet, and the things she can and cannot eat. She has also grown to accept that she cannot have the level of control that she had in her life when she was single, and she probably does eat slightly less healthily now than when we last met:

> 'It's something I struggle with because when I'm single I can just control every element of my life, and I like it, I really like it, but at the same time it's really nice being in a relationship.' (Ava: follow-up interview)

Despite the compromises that cooking a meal for two – instead of one – might entail, eating remains both a duty and a reward, a way of controlling illness and a way of caring for the body.

TWO

Exercise

'Exercise' considers the rhythms of our bodies in motion, and the complicated relationships between exercise and illness, as both a necessity and a joy. Like eating, the significance of exercise is redefined by illness, and the body is maintained, challenged and re-known through it. Exercise regimes can provide control, treatment and an alternative form of medication so that through physical activity bodies feel strong, independent and free in spite of illness. But ill bodies are prone to overexertion, and exercise can reinforce their vulnerability as well as their strength.

Exercise is an essential part of Anna's daily routine. Her day typically starts with ten touch-toe stretches, five or six holds with the head between the knees, and several touches of the hands behind the back. The movements are like a checklist, and her day will not feel right if these simple exercises are not performed. At least four times a week she does something more physically active, either running on the common or cycling through the city. Regular physical activity structures her week and works as a sort of self-medication. Not exercising, on the other hand, can have a horrible effect. Her mood will plummet quickly, and she will feel heavy, squashed somehow, penned in, trapped inside herself, irritated and annoyed. So it is vital that exercise is incorporated into her everyday life. She can easily cycle fifteen miles in a day, and the feeling of whizzing down steep hills on a bicycle is one absolutely guaranteed mood enhancing treatment, which can last five or more seconds if the hill is steep enough. In a month, she can accumulate seven hours spent running and three hundred miles cycled. A treadmill sits at home in case the weather is too bad to run outside, although it is hardly ever used because of the noise it makes (it is good for a thirty-minute run at most).

When she is running, Anna feels at peace with herself. There is something about physical exercise that stops the otherwise incessant critical commentary, the negative thoughts that trouble her mind:

> Forced myself out for a run in the amazing sun. One thing I've noticed when I run, I never worry about how far I've got to go, I just think about each step. My mind does wander but the point is with running & my cycling I

don't deploy the negative sort of constant self-evaluation & anxious anticipation that I seem to do with everything else, if I could live the way I run it would really help. The body seems able to do a lot of things without worrying about them or planning ahead; if my body was like my mind I'd be up all night worrying about how I was going to breathe in 2 weeks' time! (Anna: journal)

Ran for over an hour today. It smelt so fresh outside, how there is blossom in the air and real heat when the sun comes out. It's a very happy feeling even if I feel knackered when I get home. I like feeling physically exhausted, it's relaxing somehow. (Anna: journal)

I ran on the common for 45 minutes but it didn't really stop the spiralling thoughts whirling round in my head at the moment, only when I came over the hill and a huge blast of icy wind hit me did the monologue die down briefly … I like the exhausted feeling afterwards like having a rest from myself. (Anna: journal)

A blast of icy wind, the exhausted feeling afterwards can halt her otherwise incessant internal monologue and give Anna a rest from herself, relaxing her mind and allowing her to feel more integrated, like she is not just a mind. When she is running, there is a sort of fluidity between her mind and her body, because she thinks a lot when she is running, and it feels as if her thoughts are in tune with her movements; there is a rhythm to it. When she is really fit, it feels as though there is no effort involved at all, like she is gliding, and for ten or twenty minutes after she feels absolutely fantastic, exhausted, relaxed and ecstatic.

Anna tries to capture this feeling in her video diary, but the camera, tucked under her arm, sends the viewer lurching left and right at a heavy and heaving pace. Track underfoot and trees above swing and whirl, blurred outlines of walkers and accompanying dogs rush past, and the sound of breath working hard, regulated, keeping pace, punctuates a distant city soundscape. The resulting footage does not quite capture Anna's own experience of running, which makes her feel fluid, light and free:

Running, this is half to a third of a normal run, it lurches all over the place! (I think the 'running with camera technique' gets a bit better as I go on). The important thing is how much running helps me, and also being outside, away from my obsessive thoughts and away from noise. It's like a trip to the countryside, and all that green seems healing for me. I do think when I run, but it seems more fluid, less negative. On this run I feel better and better. (Anna: video diary)

Frustrated with the footage, Anna tries another filming technique to capture her run, asking a friend to film from a distance (so she can be seen but not identified), while she runs across the common in the mist. After, she writes a note to the camera:

Me running. Filmed by a friend. The panicky, plungey feeling from last night has gone, I feel really calm after this run. I really like running on misty, damp days as the common is much quieter; it looks beautiful in the mist. (Anna: video diary)

Later, she films her running shoes, which she alternates for each run, and her running medallions, which she has collected over many years of running. These material objects in her home help to remind her of the importance – and the joy – of running.

Alec also uses exercise as a form of medication. His regime changes all the time, but a typical week might include running three miles a day, doing weights every other day, cycling to work, taking two or three contemporary dance classes, and perhaps fitting in some swimming, yoga and Pilates too. Last summer this regime reached an Olympic training style peak, which even Alec admits was a little too much, while this summer it has been ground to a temporary halt by a hernia. But while there may be wild variations, depending on where he is and what is available there is always some sort of exercise going on (it is really frustrating, for example, that the gym does not open until 10am at weekends, when Alec wakes up at 5:30am every morning). A day or two without it and he will immediately notice a change in his mood, and the few times in the last year when there has been nothing going on at all have been very dark times. There is a symbiotic relationship between Alec's body and his soul, and he feels better or worse depending on how well he takes care of himself physically. If something causes him to miss his exercise, or if something gets him down and he does not feel like doing it, then he will not, and if he does not, then he will not be in a better mood, and he might not go to work the next day, creating a constant pressure, a background feeling of panic; nothing must slip, the momentum must be maintained.

There is no medication for Miyoshi-type muscular dystrophy. Instead, Anya tries to stay fit and healthy, like anybody, except that if she gets unfit it means that she can hardly walk. To maintain her independence and prevent the need for a wheelchair, she has also worked out what her body needs to stay strong, developing her own strengthening exercises. Swimming is one of the best things that she can do, but she also practises walking and standing exercises in the pool. Seeking advice from a physiotherapist, she found that many of the exercises she had developed herself were the same as those the physiotherapist recommended, evidence that her embodied intuition can be trusted. Working at this kind of awareness is one of the best things that Anya can do, and she compares it to the sort of physical awareness gained through the practice of martial arts or yoga. Perhaps it is an awareness that is also gained through illness. Regardless of the gradual and unhalting deterioration of her material being Anya does not separate mind from body as one might expect. Instead of fighting against her body, Anya accepts that she is her body, and she uses it to her advantage. Despite Anya's positive approach to exercise, the standard of local facilities and the practicalities of getting in the pool can make it hard to achieve as much as she would like. As she writes in her journal:

> I went to the local pool to exercise. Only one 20m lane was available and it was inevitably crowded. I doubt I'll go back to that pool. There are steps into it with a rail, but it's only one rail and without the stick one rail and slippery steps is bad news. There's a pool hoist. I'm still too proud for that. There are no stairs to access the poolside but the floors that you get there are slippery with chlorinated pool water and hair conditioner. The two or three metres between the one pool rail and one of two benches where I put my cane were difficult, nearly impossible … I walked home. I only swam for a few minutes really – couldn't do laps because of the crowd and the water was foul so I gave up and spent more time in the shower washing off the water. So, I walked home for exercise. (Anya: journal)

Ava's condition also requires her to take extra care. Rheumatoid arthritis can cause inflammation of the arteries, which increases the risk of a heart attack, so regular cardio activity is important. Lifting weights also helps; by building muscle strength she can protect her vulnerable joints from stress. Ava's day usually starts with some yoga, and she cannot sit for many hours at a time without getting stiff and needing to roll around a bit. This need or desire to get down onto the floor more than once or twice a day does not make her the ideal candidate for a nine to five job, so although it sometimes gets lonely she is happy to have the freedom and flexibility of working from home, where her yoga mat remains out on the floor and ready to be used throughout the day. She walks whenever she can, using exercise to make her body feel powerful and strong:

> This morning after I left the gym, where I had spent 30 minutes lifting some weights, all I could think of was: I want to be strong!! Even though my legs feel stronger after all of the walking, I am still so weak when it comes to lifting weight. I could only do 15 reps of leg extensions before I was too tired to continue. (Ava: journal)

In her journal, Ava also writes about her grip strength, which is affected by her arthritis. A physical therapist once measured her grip, and described it as equivalent to that of a fifty-year-old. A scene flashed before her – of living alone and not being able to open jars. So, she bought a small tub of yellow putty, to squeeze in each hand every day for several minutes. The task (which has been neglected of late) is included in a list of all the things she 'should' do daily:

1. Sleep 8 hours
2. Floss teeth (RA can also cause inflammation of the gums)
3. CARDIO – at least 20 minutes of activity which raises heart rate
4. Squeeze yellow putty for 6 minutes (increase grip strength)
5. Drink 8 glasses of water
6. Eat 5 servings of fruit + veg
7. Take B12 supplement
8. Get Omega 3s either by nuts, seeds or oily fish (but not more than 2 servings per week)

I'm sure there's more! (Ava: journal)

Aiden also has rheumatoid arthritis. It now affects his knees, feet, hands, neck, and jaw, having spread to new parts of his body over the years, but it is predominantly in his shoulders, and it makes his joints prone to pain – at any given moment he has a certain level of pain, which can easily rise to a severe, acute level if a joint becomes aggravated or inflamed. The condition makes Aiden's body weak, but it is invisible to the eye, and he looks strong, fit and healthy. To compensate for his illness, Aiden exercises. Swimming, which he normally does three times a week, is very good for his condition, because it builds up the muscles around his shoulders, the strength protecting his joints from aggravation. But Aiden's main passion is for martial arts, specifically Muay Thai (Thai Kickboxing). Kickboxing is, quite probably, the highest impact martial art that there is, so it is by his own admittance a very silly thing to do. His mum thinks he is an idiot and his doctor has told him it is not good for his body, but it is obvious how important it is to him, and he trains and fights two to three times a week. It is frustrating sometimes because he cannot push his body as far as other people can push their bodies, he cannot train as hard for a tournament and he has to take really small steps and be quite controlled about it. But training is a way of saying this is what I want to do and I am going to do it, of being in control of his body, and of choosing pain. Because, for Aiden, fighting is not about releasing his anger on others, it is about pushing his body, feeling the pain in his muscles when he does weights, and it is about getting hit – about focusing on a split lip or tasting the blood in his mouth, and knowing that the wound is going to go away in a week, and it is never going to come back and annoy him again. These injuries are something he can talk about, as he writes in his journal:

> I injured my knee earlier in the week which means I've been limping slightly since Wednesday morning. Nothing to do with my A. just happened in training: another guy's knee hit mine. It's got a deep bruise but not big as I don't really bruise that easy but it's made me realise – with a bit of embarrassment – that I actually get kinda proud of non-A. injuries. Whereas I'm quite quiet to complain or comment on pain by my A. I'm rather quick to say that I injured myself some other way not related to my condition. I don't know if it's looking to share the pain with others while avoiding the risk of judgement/sympathy – I thought I wasn't ashamed; or if it's just the fact that indirectly it's an injury by choice of mine and so I'm open to talk about it. (Aiden: journal)

Unlike arthritis, a black eye, a cut or a bruise will all heal and disappear. Exercise is, then, a mix of care and control, an attempt both to protect his body from the arthritis and to be tougher in response to it, because arthritis can be emotionally emasculating. Day-to-day activities, like grocery shopping, or taking the tube to work, can hurt, reminding Aiden of his weakness, and becoming fitter and stronger is one way to counter that.

For Anna, Alec, Anya, Ava and Aiden, exercise forms a positive relation to the body. Like disciplined eating, regular exercise is a form of dedication to the body, a way of listening to it and caring for it, and through exercise bodies become stronger and healthier in response to illness. In contrast, Adrian's exercise routine, which he captured on video, is a painful and tedious obligation. Every evening he spends half an hour performing a series of moves which are designed to work out the stiffness and soreness that has built up in his body throughout the day. Working with Thera-Bands and tennis balls, he stretches out his body, painfully massaging away the day's tensions. As he states at the end of his workout:

> All very tedious, not much fun, quite painful, but I guess that's the reality of having joint hyper-mobility syndrome. It doesn't stop me doing things, it doesn't stop me being active in any particular way … it's just that I have constant, low-level irritating pain throughout my spine, and that is generally not much fun at all. (Adrian: video diary)

Managing her body through exercise is a delicate balancing act for Amara. She grew up playing squash, basketball, running and swimming for her school, and it was not until the age of sixteen, when she still showed no signs of hitting puberty, that her parents first started to worry. Tests showed abnormally low hormone levels in her blood and she was sent for an ultrasound scan to check her internal physiology, which showed, as expected, a uterus and what seemed like ovaries. At this point it was assumed that Amara was just a late developer, and that her athleticism was delaying the onset of puberty. Only at the age of nineteen did doctors discover she is intersex. During the fourth to sixth week of gestation in her mother's womb a mutation in the Y chromosome caused a malformation of the testes, which then failed to produce testosterone and so did not trigger differentiation into the male form. Amara was born a girl but her chromosomes are XY, the male chromatic structure. This means that her body does not produce any hormones at all. Now Amara carefully manages her body, and although exercise is still important to her she has stopped working out as much as she used to, because being fit and burning fat makes her look more androgynous. She is already tall and broad; her body did not receive the signal to stop growing until she started hormone replacement therapy at nineteen; she is conscious of how big her presence is, and by exercising less she can maintain her curves and conform her body to a more feminine shape.

Exercise is a balancing act for Alice too. Diabetes and exercise are caught up in a vicious circle. Alice's sugar level initially goes up when she is exercising in the gym or swimming, because adrenalin is running through her body. But her level will then plummet at some point in the next twenty-four hours. It is difficult to know when this will happen, and it makes managing her levels a case of pure guesswork. It is likely that after exercising Alice will need to eat something, or drink some Lucozade, a need that to some extent undoes the hard work she has just put in. This in itself is enough to make mustering up the motivation to go for a swim difficult. But the situation is further complicated by the fact that going swimming involves putting on a swimming costume and revealing the bruises from her injection sites that cover her thighs. These bruises, and the physical and emotional battle of going for a swim, are pointed out to the video camera, which pans slowly along Alice's bare thigh as she draws out the tensions she feels in her body:

> I'm showing you my thigh in all its glory. I thought I should point out my bruises from my injection sites. There's one here, and then there's one here, and there's a kind of raised area here, and an area down here. I've just been for a swim, and I thought I should point out the bruises because this week I haven't gone swimming all week, because I didn't like the thought of getting in my swimming costume, and getting in the pool, and showing off my body. I know once I'm in the pool I'm not bothered by it, and no one's ever looking, and if they are I don't care, I'm kind of like well deal with it. There are plenty of women with cellulite and all sorts, so why should my body look different to theirs... And now I'm so glad I psyched myself into it, because I feel so zingy, and one of the reasons why I wanted to show you my legs, my legs and my face, is that you can see it zinging! It's just like my body is going yes! That's what you were meant to do all week, why didn't you? (Alice: video diary)

Each of these examples shows how exercise is used to strengthen and manage the body in response to illness. For the most part, exercise enables the body itself to fight back, bringing mind and body together in a shared attempt to counter illness. But exercise can also reinforce the dependence and vulnerability of the body. Sometimes, the good exercise that bodies do has repercussions that make exercising more complicated and add another source of frustration to living with illness. Apart from these dangers, there are also other more natural forms of exercise that can easily undermine the body's strength. The physical activity of making love, for instance, can hurt bodies, aggravating arthritic hip joints or causing sugar levels to plummet and allowing illness to once again rupture normality even in the most intimate moments:

> I feel I should discuss a topic which may be at the risk of sharing too much information, but bloody hell diabetes is part of my life and it does effect what I want to discuss – sex. Now as many a good diabetic nurse has informed DAFNE attendees and anyone reading some girl mag will tell you sex is excellent exercise. I know this because (well other than the obvious) my sugar levels always plummet after or even during love making. This has proved a frustrating part of my diabetes in recent years, as it completely interrupts the process, well at least it tries to. Sometimes I can feel it dropping but I am determined not to let it interrupt. I want, quite frankly, to be in control when I lose control. It's a very strange feeling to be (& here's the bit that I'm cautious to say) post-orgasm & hypoing, because it's a real mix of feeling, because in many ways it's the closest I ever get to a feeling of Zen-like hedonism. I lie there in a state of absolute bliss & I can feel my body quietly slowing down as the sugar levels drop, I find I can't move & my mouth won't form words properly & it feels good! The fact that hypos lead to bad things however means a part of my brain is going – 'Alice? Alice? Move, come on, get some Lucozade down you!' And another part is going 'what does it matter? I can just lie here, just lie here and be.' At this point I scramble around the side of the bed to find the Lucozade & glug it down. I then want to sleep, but I can't, I have to eat something, but I'm lying on a bed which I feel partially paralysed on (by this I mean it feels like trying to get up in the morning) & I'm naked. (Alice: journal)

For a moment, Alice hears her body but does not care. Her desire for complete abandon communicates an embrace of life and its pleasures regardless of the physical risks involved, and it speaks of her refusal to be confined by illness. The hypo, brought on by a severe drop in the sugar level in her blood, will make her feel dizzy and weak, and failure to react could lead to loss of consciousness and permanent physical damage. Despite these dangers, there are times when we refuse to let illness interrupt our lives.

★★★

Aiden is now happily married, and about to become a father – his wife is due to give birth in the next week. Aiden's life has settled down, and so has his rheumatoid arthritis:

> 'I used to be concerned that when I got older, trying to play, if I had a son, trying to be boisterous, would be problematic. But since it's plateaued out and started to go into remission even, it doesn't really worry me as much. There was a point there when it escalated quite quickly, and I thought with this trajectory I'm going to be fucked later on. But it's really smoothed out, so it took a lot of that anxiety away from me … I'm sure part of that is because I'm not exercising as much as I used to, I used to push my body a bit to its peak.' (Aiden: follow-up interview)

When we first met, Aiden was training regularly and practising Muay Thai, a high-impact combat sport. In the seven years that have passed, he pursued his passion to the point where his body could no longer cope:

> 'I got to a point with my hips where I just couldn't walk properly. Basically, the kickboxing, my body just said no more. My hips, I struggled to put my trousers on and stuff like that. I kept going with it, I'd go and then I'd have to wait two weeks to recover, and then I'd go again, and then I realised that I was actually just being a bit of an idiot. So I stopped and went and did just boxing, which is what I still do, and that's been more manageable. It does flare up a bit now, but I don't train as much as I used to, it's easier to manage.' (Aiden: follow-up interview)

Aiden always knew that at some point he would have to stop such a high-impact sport, but the switch, from Muay Thai to boxing, eased the disappointment of having to give training up. Aiden still feels masculine and capable – the couple renovated their house last year and Aiden did a lot of the work himself, which was tiring, but he was able to manage it. He has learned his limitations and reached a place of acceptance:

> 'I don't think it bothers me as much as it used to. I think, also, especially in my twenties, you're young and fit, excitable, you're looking forward, and you think thirty-eight is old, and beyond that is even older, and it's a bit like, oh shit. Whereas now it's ok. It's the maturity process, age stops becoming such a big deal. The arthritis being in a manageable situation just means I don't freak out about it … It's learning my own limits, carrying smaller stuff, I've just become able to manage it a lot easier and also not overcomplicate it, just accept it for what it is.' (Aiden: follow-up interview)

His awareness and acceptance of his own body, its needs, movements and limits, has grown with age, and he is now less likely to aggravate his condition:

> 'The one thing I'm used to is my movement, my range of movements now, which, there's certain stuff I can do quite easily, and stuff I can't do. I can't do angles very well. It's just like any, muscle memory or whatever they call it in dance and sport, you get used to that range and I don't deviate from it that much now. I don't accidentally lean and grab something, I don't aggravate myself. That's my world. Unless someone drops something and I react, and then I think I shouldn't have done that, I should have let the pen fall.' (Aiden: follow-up interview)

Working with his body and its limitations, Aiden has made small modifications to his everyday life. He has invested in a standing desk for his office, so that he can move between sitting and standing throughout the day, and he still regularly swims, something that he finds helps a lot. While his arthritis has settled and he has learned to live with his body and use it in different ways, prescription drugs and regular appointments with a rheumatologist are still needed to keep on top of his condition. At one point, things seemed so good that he stopped taking his pills, but after a week he was quite sore, so he went back to taking it again. As he remarked: "Loads of people take a pill every day, it's not the end of the world, I accepted that" (Aiden: follow-up interview).

Alec is now forty-one and has made a family, having adopted a son and met a new partner. The three live together with their pet dog in a flat in London. The dramatic highs and lows of life with bipolar disorder followed Alec through the long and demanding adoption process (two and a half years from the first phone call to being matched with a child), but since his son arrived life has been a little calmer and he is still medication-free (the good of it never outweighed the side effects). The family hope to move to another country, somewhere where the weather is better, in the next few years. Still, it is important not to forget that bipolar remains a part of Alec's everyday life:

> 'I would say that it is a part of my life still … you can be lulled into a false sense of security over these things and that's a mistake, when you think everything's going great, with a relationship and a child and stuff like that you think everything's going great and then it gets out of hand sometimes and so it's better to be thinking about it than not.'
> (Alec: follow-up interview)

Finding the time to exercise has been difficult, but all the things that need to be done when you have a child have, in a way, replaced that need. Alec's son is now the centre of his routine:

> 'I think having a child has been really good because there's a routine, and that routine holds me as much as it holds him; there's certain things that have to be done and there's no question about it and they have to be done at the same time every single day, and you let go of that at your peril … Everyday life is just both what I crave, the comfort of the routine of everyday life, and it is also just, I think always going to be a bafflement to me.'
> (Alec: follow-up interview)

There are times when Alec finds it hard to keep on top of everyday things, like changing the sheets and making sure there are clean clothes, or preparing lunch, and he still feels the temptation to let his life spiral out of control. There are also times when it is harder to keep to the routine. Holidays, for example, break up routines, and as much as Alec looks forward to them he also finds them disruptive and difficult to manage. Perhaps what has been hardest is telling his new partner and son about his condition, and seeing them live through the ups and downs with him:

> 'No amount of telling someone up-front can really prepare them for what it looks like in reality. And then when that happens it's like, you know it does wear people out and so that's sad and it's hard but we've reached a way of working now.'
> (Alec: follow-up interview)

There are certain things Alec has put in place, and he hopes that as he grows older he will see that those things are not a choice, that they are not optional for him. For example, he has to eat breakfast, it helps to write in his journal, and the family dog also plays an important role:

> 'When I'm at optimal healthiness I get up very early in the morning and I write some good pages and then eat breakfast and pray and meditate, and that's optimum functioning.'
> (Alec: follow-up interview)

> 'The dog was a big deal I have to say. I call her a therapy animal, just stroking her ... The arguments lowered when she came. You can take her out for a walk, take her to the back garden, it's an excuse to get out, so that was really helpful actually.'
> (Alec: follow-up interview)

THREE

Sleep

'Sleep' looks at how the demands of our working and social lives can conflict with the demands of our body, and how illness redefines our lives through the need to sleep. While rest is sometimes the best cure for illness, sleep clashes with social expectations, destroys busy routines and causes conflicts. The need to sleep is perhaps the most delicate revelation of the body's vulnerability.

Anna's depression makes her want to sleep, slowing her down and making her feel tired and heavy:

> 'My body feels really different when I am depressed. It feels so heavy, which is a bit of a paradox having talked about feeling light and out of my body, but at the same time it's feeling heavy, not being able to, losing fluidity, just wanting to sleep all the time, not wanting to wake up, a sort of hangover feeling from sleeping so much or just from being depressed, I don't know which. It's a real slowing down for me.' (Anna: interview)

During these slow times, Anna will return to bed, not so much because she wants to sleep but because she doesn't want to be awake. Together with depression, Anna also suffers from insomnia and sporadic sleep disturbance. The word insomnia is logged six times in her journal, which she kept for one month, and her sleepless nights are captured on video. The camera is in night vision mode, fixed on Anna's eye as she lies restlessly in bed. Her note to the camera reads:

> Eye at night. (I like it upside down and the other-worldly green hue.) I'm feeling quite flat and pointless, it's been building up since this afternoon. An irrational thought is floating around inside me, based on nothing more than a flash of intuition. I don't want to go into it, as it's probably nonsense, but I think it's making me feel an unpleasant emptiness that is very familiar. It's important to stay in the moment with this feeling and not follow a trail of stories. To locate it in my body I would say it's a nauseous flutter in my stomach. I'm having

anxious and slightly hopeless thoughts about the future.
(Anna: video diary)

Negative thoughts often keep Anna awake, spinning around in her head when she is most vulnerable to them, and lack of sleep later contributes to her gloomy mood, leaving her feeling tired and lacking in motivation during the day:

> I fell asleep reading this afternoon, it's the insomnia catching up with me, it leaves me very flat & low, wiped out and lacking enthusiasm. Really drained. Don't feel good about myself, feel like I am a stupid waste of space; that's the sort of thing my therapist would say is not me speaking but other voices I shouldn't allow in. It's hard not to allow in the idea that everything I do is wrong at the moment. The physical exhaustion I'm feeling today adds to the feeling that I can't cope with things very well and screw things up. (Anna: journal)

Together, depression and insomnia turn sleep into a problem for Anna's body, and the link between not having enough sleep and feeling depressed means that sleep is both hard to find and really important. Her recurring dreams haunt her mind, and emphasise the strength of her body:

> Dreamt last night I was clinging onto a cliff face trying not to fall into a violent sea. It's a variation on a recurring dream I've had for about 30 years, trying not to fall or be knocked from a cliff, usually into the sea or a fast-flowing river. I have to rely on all my physical strength to save myself, if this was really how I could protect myself I don't think I'd ever get depressed. (Anna: journal)

Like Anna, Amelia suffers from depression together with insomnia and distressed sleep. Bad periods of depression affect her sleeping patterns, and make her want to sleep throughout the afternoons. These are times when life stops happening, and days and weeks cannot be remembered. They are marked by apathy, and stand out in contrast to the times when she is kept busy and active with work. Sometimes her body feels light, and can achieve what she wants it to do; these are times when she is confident about her potentials – if not in life, career or future, then as a person, managing to survive. But at other times Amelia feels too unhealthy and foggy to get anything done, even sitting at the computer, and certainly not going outside, because that would be too difficult. It is as though the world is projected onto her and her body does not have the agency to perform the tasks that it has the potential to do; instead she feels heavy, tired, low, apathetic, hopeless, tormented and stuck. The fluctuation between these two states, marked by lightness and heaviness, reveals the co-dependent relationship between Amelia's mind and her body; her state of mind affects her body so much, and vice versa, that her body can make her feel heavy or light in her mind. But it is not that Amelia's body betrays her, or that she does not trust her body, which changes so much; rather it is that sometimes she does not do it justice. A bad nights' sleep, a night of teeth grinding and distress, leaves her feeling tired and in turn affects her stomach; either she will not eat enough, or she will eat too much, or the wrong thing, and this combined with feeling bad and not having slept means that a lot of the time she feels quite shaky or empty, and therefore not healthy enough to go outside and achieve things.

Alice's nights are also often disturbed. In order to fend off a night-time hypo she can drink some Lucozade or eat a crumpet before going to bed, but these measures do not always prevent her blood glucose level dropping while she is sleeping, triggering a hypo which will then wake her up:

> 'When you have a night-time hypo, it's different for people, sometimes you can sleep through one, and your body will find a natural reserve in itself, but that's a dangerous thing to let it do. It's quite scary to have a night-time hypo. Interestingly my body usually wakes me up; it incorporates it into a dream. You can feel it, it starts to come through in the dream, the feeling is kind of, well it varies; in my case I find that I shake a lot, it's like fainting, a very sluggish feeling, also I stumble over my words terribly, I really stutter.' (Alice: interview)

One of these interrupted nights is captured on video. In the video, Alice describes the sensation of being woken by a hypo, checks her blood glucose level, and tries to work out the chain of events that have led to this moment. A bedside light dimly lights the room and shines on Alice, who is lying in bed, eyes half open, her voice soft and slightly quivering. Her head is resting on a white pillow and her arm is outstretched, holding the camera out in front of her so that she can speak to it. At this moment, I am looking at her, but it also feels like she is looking at me, showing me, bringing me into her night through the camera. She decides to check her blood glucose level, not because she needs to check it but because she wants to show me the evidence, the reason why her night has been ruptured. The sheets rustle as she moves around in bed, and the camera swings round with her body before coming to rest on the bed sheets, leaving her hands free to perform the test. A quick click to the tip of her middle finger, which she then holds to the blood glucose monitor, it reads 3.4 (under the normal low of 4). Both Alice and the camera swing round again so that she can lie down, tired, frustrated and confused. The minutes pass as Alice tries to figure out the cause of this drop, and as she works through the possibilities her voice becomes steadier, clearer, brighter. The hypo is fading, leaving her hungry and needing the loo, but instead of climbing out of bed she smiles, turns the light and the camera off, and drifts back to sleep. Alice's narrative runs over this sequence:

I don't know what time it is, I've just woken up in the middle of the night, a few minutes ago. My top lip tingles, and I'm clearly hypoing but I don't know what my sugar level is, it was 9.8 when I went to bed, which is fine. I've hypoed a lot lately. Anyway, I just drunk what was by my bedside without even thinking, which was half a bottle of lemon Lucozade. So, I'm just waiting for it to come up. My top lip still feels a bit dead, but it definitely feels like it's getting there. I feel kind of like tingly around my head, around my fingers, which is always a sign. I don't even know what my level is, I probably should check it. In fact, I'll film it and check it. I don't really check in the middle of the night when I hypo, because why else would I wake up in the middle of the night, other than because my sugar level has dropped. Let's find out. This is after drinking the Lucozade, yes, its 3.4. This happened last night … It must be my background insulin, because, what's the time? The time is 1:30am. Is that all? I wish it was later. I went to bed this evening because I felt really tired after hypoing last night. After hypoing last night, I felt really tired the next day, because I'd gone to bed late and then hypoed, and had to get up at like 6:45am … This is a horribly rambled message, isn't it? I thought I should take you through how my brain works, when I'm hypoing in the middle of the night. Anyway, funnily enough, I can feel my top lip has stopped tingling, just about, and there isn't the general feeling of tinnitus which happens when I hypo, at night anyway, that's disappeared; at 1:34am, that's how I'm feeling. The problem is I'm really hungry; it's probably just my body going feed me, eat sugar, but if I do that, I mean I've already had enough sugar now to raise my sugar level to around 10 tomorrow morning, so I can't really eat anything … Anyway, I'm going to go back to sleep: night night. (Alice: video diary)

For Ava and Aiden sleeping well is a preventative measure. Getting a good amount of sleep every night helps their bodies rest and recuperate, and, vice versa, not getting enough sleep means that their conditions are more likely to flare up and cause problems. It seems straightforward, but getting eight hours sleep every night is actually quite hard. Social pressures and the demands of work mean that sleep has to be defended:

> 'it's very easy to only sleep six hours during the week, and really that's not enough for me, but it's quite hard to get eight hours every night. So, it's almost like I had to learn to give myself permission to sleep eight or nine hours. Some people think that's so much, because everybody is so busy, and especially when you're young, you should be out having fun and staying up until four in the morning, so then to actually get a proper eight hours of sleep, it's so hard to fight for.' (Ava: interview)

While defending the need to sleep or stay in bed is hard, ignoring this need has directly felt consequences. Lack of sleep quickly leads to general tiredness, increased levels of pain, exhaustion and bad moods:

> Not much to say; same deal as usual, wake up (always tired) have a day with niggles and pains still mainly in my shoulders and hips but my neck and feet have something to say also. (Aiden: journal)

> Quite knackered by the end of this week – just doing too much and not getting enough sleep. Too little sleep means that I'm pretty sore today: nowhere in particular generally just all the affected joints. So, a lot of pain today has put me in a bad/snappy mood. (Aiden: journal)

The need to get an early night, to refuse social engagements or to leave early is in itself a reminder of the frailty of their bodies, and it is one that transports illness from the body into social situations that, like bodies, have to be dealt with. Keeping up with the pace of modern life is a recipe for disaster, highlighting the tension that exists between the body and society. There is simply no space for the needs of ill bodies when it comes to employment, for example:

> Too much. I was lying in bed fighting to will myself out of bed. The pain is there, and usually pretty bad in the mornings anyway, but it's the fatigue. Your body feels as though it's submerged in sand and every effort requires too much effort. I was lying in bed, not after a late night – just recent physical activity, and my body was screaming for sleep to rest and rejuvenate. Rest works better than any drug but with a modern life in London it's the hardest thing to come by. Lying in bed after numerous 'snoozes' I'm thinking if I was ill, like with a cold or gastro or whatever I could call work and say I'm not well enough to come in, but I can't (or is it won't) call to say my A. won't allow me to get to work. I could say I'd be late but then people stop depending on you – you get put in the faulty basket. Knackered …
> (Aiden: journal)

For April, being stressed and tired is a trigger for a night time seizure, leading to further lack of sleep and exhaustion. April discovered that she has epilepsy when she was eleven years old. Lying in bed one night on holiday in a foreign country, she suddenly woke up. Her whole body was rigid, moving, out of control. She tried to speak, to call out for help, but nothing came out. She lost consciousness. Waking up for a second time she wondered if it had been a bad dream, but then the first of what was to become many epileptic seizures took hold of her. The third time she woke up she found herself in an ambulance, on her way to hospital. Sometime after this event April's condition was medically diagnosed: she has an unusual form of epilepsy, manifesting in nocturnal seizures that occur between shallow and deep sleep. The diagnosis was difficult to reach – MRI (magnetic resonance imaging) and EEG (electroencephalogram) tests, which create pictures of the brain and record its electrical activity, failed to reveal the condition because you cannot see it unless it is happening in the moment. Several weeks spent in hospital eventually allowed doctors to see the symptoms and to make the diagnosis.

As a child, seizures only ever happened at night, when April was asleep. Night-time seizures are especially dangerous, because it is possible to lose consciousness without realising. But the fact that they only happened at night offered April invisibility; just as the condition had been invisible to medical tests, it was also invisible to April's friends, and there was no need to tell anyone about her condition unless she wanted to spend a night away from home. As she grew older, and stayed up later, the seizures inevitably began to invade April's evenings. April cannot trust her body when she is tired, and going out at night is now a risk: 'I'm meant to be going out this evening and to be honest I don't trust my body to cope' (April: journal).

The need to run on her body's time is perhaps one of the most annoying features of living with epilepsy:

> I'm on my way home to ensure the tiredness/stress of a busy week doesn't get to me. That's what annoys me about having a long term illness; you have to take these 'preventative' measures into account in daily life. (April: journal)

Other seemingly small details that can disrupt the sleeping body and trigger pain include the beds, mattresses and pillows that we sleep on. Adrian has joint hypermobility syndrome, a long-term inherited genetic disorder that affects the collagen in his ligaments, making them too stretchy and weak to provide the strong scaffolding required to hold skeleton and muscles firmly together. This means that his joints go through a greater range of movement than they should do, overextending his body. In most people, it causes no pain whatsoever; the only symptom is increased flexibility. But for a small subset of those people, the condition is not a party trick; instead, it is a significant cause of pain. Adrian has inherited a suboptimal set of bones and muscles, and they hurt. Every morning when he wakes up his back has already started hurting. In an attempt to improve his sleep, Adrian has purchased a mattress and pillows that should offer his body the right support. All the same, he simply never wakes up with his back feeling like it has been rested:

> 5.32am Alarm goes off as normal. Snooze applied as normal …
> 5.37am Alarm goes off for real. Get up, drink water, feeling stiff in lower back. No idea whether it's my bed or my back or my pillow combination, but I simply cannot ever wake up with my back feeling like it's been

rested. I toss and turn most of the night, every night, every time because my body doesn't feel right, doesn't feel comfortable. (Adrian: journal)

This situation is made worse if Adrian is sleeping away from home. A work trip or a holiday is guaranteed to mean an uncomfortable bed, poor sleep and increased pain, as he describes in his journal:

2nd–9th April – Holiday in Cornwall
A very welcome break from the routine. We've got a cottage booked. My first longer break away from home for more than 2 years. I wonder how my hypermobility will be affected?

Bed
The cottage is wonderful, all mod cons and the kids love it. Two problems occur to me after the first night. First, the bed is tiny, I'm guessing 4' 6", without duvet just lots of heavy blankets. Second, the bed is really, really uncomfortable. I could feel every spring under my back, and woke up each morning with a very sore lower back. That said, I have a lesser version of this problem at home with what is a 6' mattress and supposedly one offering just the right support. I would love to wake up one morning and not feel some part of my spinal region aching. (Adrian: journal)

Each of these examples shows how the sleeping body lies at the heart of everyday life with illness. The basic need to sleep underscores our lives, and bodies that need to sleep more, or more comfortably, than others simply do not fit in with the demands of modern life. As such, they present themselves as things that demand care, that are frail and difficult to manage.

★★★

Sleep was always important for both Aiden and Ava, and while some things in life have changed, and other things are just about to change, sleep has not lost its power with the passage of time:

> 'One thing that I'm still quite aware of is rest. It's always been a main thing that I need sleep to recover, and now, even though I get seven hours a night, I don't top up on the weekends. When I was a bit younger and I had less responsibility, I used to sleep six or seven hours during the working week and then I'd have massive sleeps on the weekend, but I don't do that anymore, I guess that's why I feel quite tired and it gets me a bit achy. So, I'm just waiting to see what it's like when there's a kid around! I'm going to lack sleep, so wait and see, maybe I will rest in different ways.' (Aiden: follow-up interview)

> 'The past six years I really have felt so liberated from any idea of being unwell, which has been great, and every now and then I feel slightly in my joints a bit like I haven't been taking care of myself in a way, and I imagine sometimes if I were to test my blood or inflammation levels then it would be slightly elevated because I can feel if I am abusing myself by working too hard or I'm not sleeping, or my feet will really start to hurt. I feel like I'm just so in tune with my body that I can feel all of these very subtle changes, and lately things have been so busy with work that I started to feel a bit, okay if I'm not careful and if I keep going like this then there could be some kind of recurrence. But then I just sleep a lot. I feel like I'm almost like some kind of mammal that hibernates, I can just go into my shell and repair myself.' (Ava: follow-up interview)

No one knows what the future holds, but Ava and her partner are also starting to think about having children. Like Aiden, her biggest concern is the impact that being pregnant and caring for a baby could have on her need for sleep:

> 'It terrifies me, what if I get pregnant and I am just tired for nine months? ... So those things scare me, because like I said sleep has been really important. The fact that I can sleep has been an amazing thing, and to have that threatened really scares me.' (Ava: follow-up interview)

1. Polaroid of Ava's hands

2. Polaroid of Anya's legs

3. Polaroid of Anya's legs

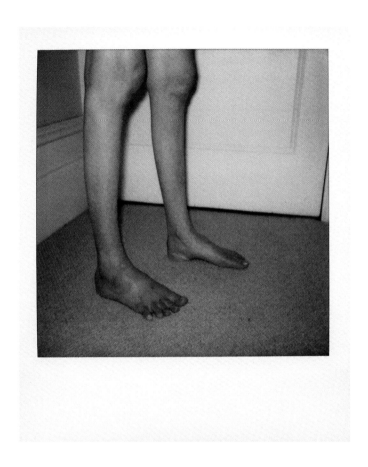

4. Walking stick by Anya

This is my stick. I use it quite a bit. I'm glad this isn't a picture of a wheelchair. No offence to wheelchair users.

5. RIP pancreas by Alice

one day my pancreas
decided to give up. Ever
since I'm not allowd to

6. Aiden's journal

Nothing out of the ordinary happening:
That is a general feeling of tightness
in my joints especially my shoulders -
as always - and my knees at the
moment. I always notice my knees
going down the escalators to the tube,
morning & evening. My neck is stiff
but I'm assuming most people who
sit in front of a computer for
10 hours a day have a stiff neck
(I'm sure cheap IKEA mattresses don't
help) so I don't know if my neck
is any sorer than that of the guy
next to me.

I'm generally quite aware of my
A. and how it affects my body but
since receiving this journal and not
knowing what to write about, I've

paid a little more attention to my joints. And My shoulders seem to have a little rythm of their own. My Right shoulder will be the main source of pain / uncomfortable till about 15:00 and then it'll swap swap with the left shoulder — dunno why.

People who I sit near at work have accepted me stretching my shoulders on my desk. Every now and then they'll comment on how it looks painful. It's actually very relieving.

Some times people will comment on my pill — I put one Celebrex capsule on my key board every morning to remind my self to take it after lunch. I used to hide the taking of my pill but that meant that I sometimes forgot (not worth being discreet for the sake of people I work with).

When people do comment I'll usually say jokingly "It makes the pain go away" not completely true but they'll be a little confused and smile or I answer sincerely and say it's an anti inflamatory for my A. to this people will either be quiet and / or a little awkward or they will ask further — which is fine — ultimately they will say / ask if I'm too young for A. No.

Speaking of pills, I just took my last today, last of a box at 60.

of the R.A. Which can be incredibly discouraging + frustrating. I suppose it's much easier to make sacrifices when you are promised – or guaranteed – results. But when you are making sacrifices + you still feel swollen in your hands, you wonder why you are bothering... So I am still working out how many indulgences to allow myself and really for me I don't think there is one set answer. I think it's a matter of constantly monitoring how swollen I feel and knowing when to be more careful. Sometimes I do wonder if anybody else ever feels swollen in their joints. or stiff when they wake up. It is such an individual, subjective sensation. Which makes it ridiculous, when you think about it, how doctors expect to understand whether you are better off or worse off than your last appointment. Which is why I suppose they sometimes use the number scale. Can you rate your pain from 1 to 10? Things like that. But for me it's never PAIN, it's just PRESENCE. Some days I am extremely aware of my fingers that I feel big and fat and unfeminine. And some days I'm aware of my feet, my toes especially, which just ache. And some days when I feel that tension has built up in my shoulders and I roll my head around to relieve it, I hear what sounds to me like the crunch of crinoline on an evening dress which I'm not sure if it's the R.A. or not. I think I always forget to ask. And sometimes I don't forget but don't bother because I am not in the mood to not get an answer because what I have learned is that there are no answers with autoimmune diseases. They make themselves known to the person they are affecting, but are often elusive and evasive to the doctors and especially in laboratory tests. A few months ago I had low white blood

I was to squeeze every day in each hand for several minutes. The good news is that it travelled all the way from NY with me. The bad news is that I had to dig it out of my closet yesterday. I may re-start that today. Though again, if I were to make a list of all the things I SHOULD do daily, I wouldn't have time for anything or anyone else.

Things I 'should' do daily:

① Sleep 8 hours

② Floss Teeth - R.A. can also cause inflammation of the gums

③ CARDIO - at least 20 minutes of activity which raises heart rate

④ Squeeze yellow putty for 6 minutes (increase grip strength)

⑤ Drink 8 glasses of water

⑥ Eat 5 servings of fruit + veg

⑦ Take B-12 supplement

⑧ Get omega 3s either by nuts, seeds or oily fish (but not more than 2 servings per week)

I'm sure there's more!

And then there's the not so positive list:

① AVOID (or in my case, don't overindulge in):

    CAFFEINE

    SUGAR

    ALCOHOL

    RED MEAT - not a problem for me

    DAIRY - not a problem for me

There's also some question as to whether citrus fruits + vegetables in the nightshade family cause/aggravate inflammation

② Watch your saturated fat intake

③ And above all, don't get stressed!

Things I am

12 stone
dis organised
poorly motivated
an Hb1aC of 8.2
bad at changing needles regularly
perhaps paranoid of hypoing
happy & greatful for the people around me

concerned for my future
determined to not let it rule me
even though its a loosing battle

Things that are meant to happen to me if I don't keep 'good control'

- blind
- kidney failure
- stroke
- heart attacks
- gangrene
- numb (in feet & hands)
- produce sick children
- don't produce children
- depression
- no sex drive

Things I am meant to do

write down my sugar levels
write down what I eat & its carb count
weigh my food
exercise regularly
change the needle after each injection
keep cotton wall in my blood tester kit
check sugar only at meals
        exercise
        bed
        or when feeling hyper
inject for every carb portion I eat over 1.
→ breakfast
→ lunch
→ dinner
→ snacks

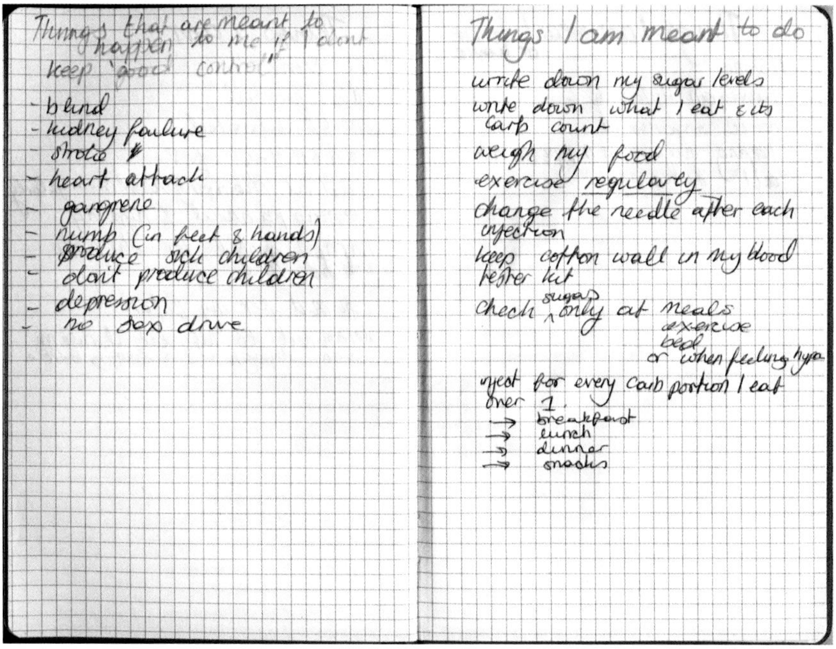

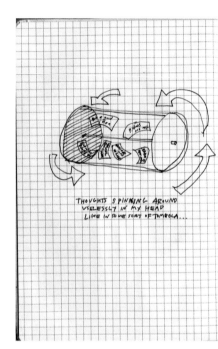

THOUGHTS SPINNING AROUND
USELESSLY IN MY HEAD
LIKE IN SOME SORT OF TOMBOLA...

06/03/09

TWO AND A HALF PANIC ATTACKS
THIS WEEK. A FUNNY WAY TO START
A JOURNAL, BUT AT LEAST BY THE END
PART OF THE WEEK I'D REMEMBERED
SOME OF THE THINGS I'VE BEEN TAUGHT.
TO GET SOME KIND OF A GRIP AT THE
ONSET OF A PANIC

THE FIRST PANIC ATTACK OF THE WEEK (ON
MONDAY) IS TOO HORRIBLE FOR ME TO WRITE
ABOUT IN DETAIL. I DON'T THINK ANYONE
ELSE WOULD HAVE NOTICED, THOUGH THERE
WERE LOADS OF PEOPLE AROUND ME [THE
REASON FOR THE ANXIETY IN THE FIRST PLACE].
THE MAIN PHYSICAL SENSATIONS WERE:
A) JUST NOT 'FEELING 'IN' MY BODY, WEIRDLY
UNGROUNDED, UNSTABLE
B) CONVINCED I WOULD BREAKDOWN OR
SOMEHOW DISINTEGRATE

DON'T UNDERSTAND WHY I FORGOT
WHAT TO DO. JUST HAPPENS SOMETIMES I
SUPPOSE. LEFT ME FEELING A BIT SHAKY
AND ANNOYED WITH MYSELF

SECOND PANIC ATTACK, YESTERDAY, I SOME-
HOW 'CAUGHT', SUDDENLY HAD AN INSIGHTFUL
VIEW OF MYSELF AND SAW I WAS SHAKING
& COLD, NAUSEOUS. REMEMBERED TO ALLOW
MYSELF TO FEEL WHAT WAS HAPPENING IN
MY BODY. TO PLACE BOTH MY FEET ON THE
GROUND, BREATHE SLOWLY. ACKNOWLEDGE
THIS DREADED, FRIGHTENED FEELING IN MY
CHEST AND GUT, WEAKNESS IN MY HANDS.
THEN I VISUALISED AN IMMENSE LANDSCAPE.

13. Anna's journal

07/03/09

TYPICAL START TO THE DAY:

1) STRETCH, TOUCH TOES 10 TIMES

2) HEAD BETWEEN KNEES, TRY TO HOLD
   5 OR 6 TIMES

3) TOUCH HANDS BEHIND BACK SEVERAL
   TIMES.

THIS IS LIKE A CHECKLIST. THE DAY
WONT FEEL RIGHT IF THESE THINGS ARENT
DONE.

TODAY: CYCLED 15 MILES

TRIED TO FOCUS ON SELF-SUFFICIENCY
OF CYCLING, THINKING OF SOMETHING
MY THERAPIST SAID YESTERDAY, FELT A
BIT CONTRIVED. THOUGH I DO FEEL
THE MOST SENSE OF CONTENTMENT WHEN
CYCLING OR RUNNING. INFACT ITS THE
ONLY TIME I REALLY GET IT - THE
IDEA OF BEING AT PEACE WITH ONES SELF,
ACTUALLY FEEL IT. OH THAT SEEMS A BIT

MY BELOVED BICYCLE

SELF-PITYING. I DONT MEAN IT DRAMATICALLY.

JUST SOMETHING ABOUT PHYSICAL EXERCISE
THAT STOPS THE OTHERWISE INCESSANT CRITICAL
COMMENTARY....

✻ NOT ANXIOUS   ✻ SPENT DAY WITH OTHERS & ONCE 2HR)

08/03/09

ONE MINOR MOOD PLUNGE. CAN'T EXACTLY
RATIONALISE. WENT WITH A FRIEND TO
SEE THE GERHARD RICHTER PORTRAITS. FELT
I WAS ANNOYING HER WITH MY PRESENCE.
HOME NOW AND FEELING FLAT & POINTLESS
THIS IS ACCOMPANIED BY A SORT OF WEAK,
DRAINED FEELING IN MY HANDS, STOMACH
AND FEET. I'M MENTIONING THAT BECAUSE
I KNOW ITS ONE OF THE THEMES OF THIS RESEARCH, BUT
ITS ALSO A WAY I'VE BEEN SHOWN IN THERAPY
TO EXPERIENCE THINGS, WITHOUT PILING ON A
LOT OF STORIES TO THE MOMENT - SUCH AS
SAYING I'M "POINTLESS" - A GOOD EXAMPLE OF
PROJECTING NEGATIVE MEANINGS ONTO WHAT
I'M FEELING. THE LITTLE MOOD PLUNGE
IS CHARACTERISED ABOVE ALL BY A LACK OF
ENERGY AND A LOSS OF FOCUS.
GENERALLY OVER THE LAST FEW MONTHS
I'VE BEEN FEELING LESS DEPRESSED (A
LOT LESS) BUT A LOT MORE ANXIOUS. INSTEAD
AS IF THINGS HAVE SHIFTED FROM MY MIND
TO MY BODY. AS ANXIETY IS SO VISCERAL,
ITS HARDER TO HIDE FROM OTHER PEOPLE.
WISH I'D HAD TIME FOR A RUN TODAY, AS
I KNOW THAT WOULD MAKE THINGS BETTER,
& I'D FEEL BETTER ABOUT MYSELF - I
KNOW THIS FROM SEVEN YEARS OF REGULAR
RUNNING. SO I'LL DO THAT TOMORROW.
✻ DOWN BUT NOT ANXIOUS! ✻ SPENT AM WITH FRIEND

I'M NOT SURE IF THE INCESSANT WORRIED VOICES ARE PART OF A DEPRESSIVE MINDSET. MAYBE OTHER PEOPLE ARE LIKE THAT WHO HAVE NEVER EXPERIENCED A SEVERE DEPRESSION. THERE'S SOMETHING NIBBLING AWAY AT ME AT THE MOMENT, A LITTLE RAT, NOT THE SHARK ATTACK OF A SIGNIFICANT DEPRESSION. IT JUST MEANS THERE'S A LITTLE SOMETHING MAKING ME FEEL 'WRONG' OR BAD ABOUT MYSELF. A REMINDER I'M NOT GOOD ENOUGH. I'M TRYING TO REMIND MYSELF THAT THOSE ARE JUST INVADING THOUGHTS, STORIES & HABITS. I SHOULD PROBABLY 'MEDITATE, BUT AM TOO LAZY AND PREFER TO WATCH SHIT ON TV. BUT MEDITATION CAN REALLY HELP WITH THIS MADDENING BABBLE. I'M NERVOUS ABOUT WORKING TOMORROW. BY THE EVENING I'LL BE FINE I'M SURE. IT'S A PATTERN I'VE GOT INTO. I'LL HAVE INSOMNIA TONIGHT AND THE THOUGHTS OF HOW DREAD-FULL EVERYTHING IS GOING TO BE WILL GO ROUND & ROUND. THEN IT WILL BE MEDIOCRE TV OR K I'LL GO HOME WONDERING WHY ON EARTH I LET THINGS GET TO ME SO BADLY. (UNLESS EVERY-THING DOES GO TERRIBLY WRONG OF COURSE). IT'S SO PREDICTABLE, YOU'D THINK I SHOULD JUST BE ABLE TO GET A GRIP AND STOP.

WHIZZ

WHIZZING DOWN STEEP HILLS ON A BICYCLE IS THE ONE ABSOLUTELY GUARANTEED MOOD ENHANCING TREATMENT. CAN LAST UPTO FIVE OR MORE SECONDS IF THE HILL IS STEEP ENOUGH. I DO THIS ABOUT 9 TIMES A WEEK ON MY JOURNEYS ROUND SOUTH LONDON.

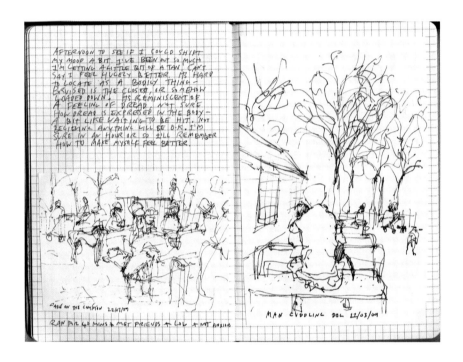

I RUN PAST THESE TREES
SEVERAL TIMES A WEEK, IN THE
LAST WEEK AND A HALF
IT'S BECOME INTOXICATING
LOOKING AT THEM FEELS
BENEFICIAL, IT'S A BOOST TO
MY MIND BEING IN THEIR PRESENCE.
I'VE BEEN DRAWING & PHOTOGRAPHING
THEM FOR NEARLY 25 YEARS.

THEY FEEL LIKE A REALLY POSITIVE
PART OF MY LIFE & ROUTINES,
WHEN THINGS AREN'T GOING VERY
WELL OR I'M FEELING SHIT ABUT
MYSELF ITS REALLY IMPORTANT/USEFULL
TO ANCHOR MYSELF IN THINGS LIKE THESE
TREES OR THE BUSHES OF THE LANDSCAPE A
FEW HUNDRED YARDS FROM MY HOME.

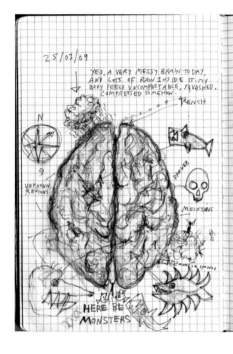

25/03/09

YES, A VERY MESSY BRAIN TODAY,
AND LOTS OF RAIN INSIDE IT. MY
BODY FEELS UNCOMFORTABLE, SQUASHED.
COMPRESSED SOMEHOW.

N

UNKNOWN REGIONS

TRENCH

DANGER

MOUNTAINS

HERE BE
MONSTERS

RAN ON MY TREADMILL FOR THIRTY MINUTES (AS
MUCH AS I COULD STAND OF THE NOISE).
THE WEATHER IS A BIT RAINY ON AND
OFF, WHICH IS MY EXCUSE FOR STAYING
INDOORS. BUT I JUST DONT FEEL UP FOR IT
TODAY. I DONT FEEL LIKE SEEING ANYONE
ELSE. I FEEL FRAGILE. SOMETIMES I'M
VERY CONFIDENT AND COMFORTABLE WITH OTHERS
BUT OTHER TIMES I CAN'T EVEN LOOK AT
THEM. ITS ALMOST AS IF I FEEL INFERIOR
TO OR JUDGED BY OTHERS. TODAY SEEMS LIKE
ONE OF THOSE DAYS (THOUGH I HAVEN'T SEEN
ANYONE ELSE TO ACTUALLY TEST THIS OUT). IT
MIGHT BE A BIT OF A LOOP, BECAUSE THE
LONGER I HIDE MYSELF AWAY THE HARDER IT
GETS TO FACE PEOPLE. BUT I REALLY HAVE
GOT GOOD AT 'FORCING' MYSELF OUT. I'M LUCKY
MY MODE OF WORKING SUPPORTS THESE PHASES
(I SUPPOSE OTHERS MIGHT THINK ITS UNFORT-
UNATE THAT IT ISN'T CHALLENGED) BUT I'VE
PUT MYSELF INTO MUCH MORE CHALLENGING
SITUATIONS OVER THE LAST COUPLE OF YEARS,
FROM BEING IN A SITUATION WHERE I HARDLY
EVER WENT OUT, OR AROUND OTHER PEOPLE, I'M
NOW DOING IT FOR WORK + REASONS ON A REGULAR
BASIS. BUT TODAY IS NOT ONE OF THOSE DAYS!

WRITING THIS JOURNAL HAS HELPED ME TO RECOGNISE
SOME OF THE WAYS IN WHICH I HAVE CHANGED. I
DONT THINK I'M DELUDING MYSELF BY SEEING THEM
AS POSITIVE. THERE ARE LOTS OF AREAS FOR
IMPROVEMENT STILL, I KNOW THAT! I'D LIKE TO FEEL:

* A LOT LESS ANXIOUS
* MORE CONFIDENT ABOUT MY WORK
* LESS THREATENED BY OTHER PEOPLE

I'm doing a tidy up, so if you see the mess in my room ignore that, but I've just counted the amount of Lucozade that I've found in my bin, probably, if I'm quite honest, 3 months, so January through to March, that's probably not all of it really. So that's 6 weeks' worth, its 22 bottles, that doesn't include the glucose tablets I have, or the bottles that I've left at my boyfriend's place or taken in the street. Quite an array, as you can see. (Alice: video diary)

18. Injecting insulin/ 19. Lucozade

I'm showing you my thigh in all its glory, I thought I should point out my bruises from my injection sites. There's one here, and then there's one here, and there's a kind of raised area here, and an area down here. I've just been for a swim, and I thought I should point out the bruises because this week I haven't gone swimming all week… (Alice: video diary)

I don't really check in the middle of the night when I hypo, because why else would I wake up in the middle of the night, other than because my sugar level has dropped. Let's find out. (Alice: video diary)

20. Bruised thigh/ 21. Checking sugar level at night

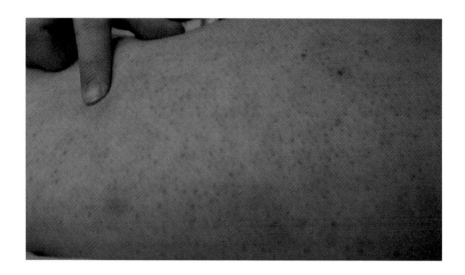

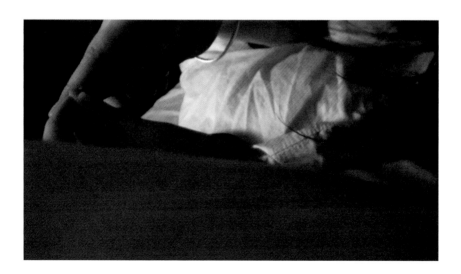

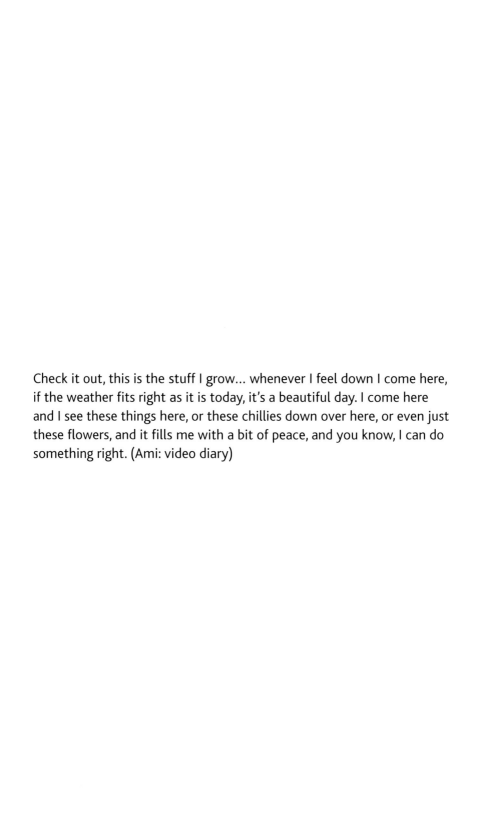

Check it out, this is the stuff I grow... whenever I feel down I come here, if the weather fits right as it is today, it's a beautiful day. I come here and I see these things here, or these chillies down over here, or even just these flowers, and it fills me with a bit of peace, and you know, I can do something right. (Ami: video diary)

22. Tomato plant/ 23. Cherry tomato

Night shot. My eye. Upside down like my thoughts. I'm trying to get to sleep but can't because my thoughts are spinning round. (Anna: video diary)

24. Eye at night / 25. Jellyfish

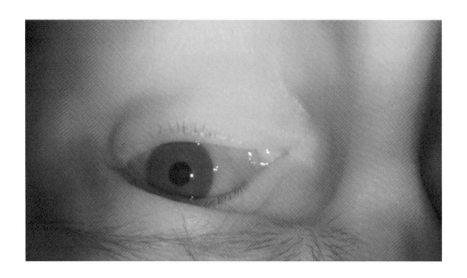

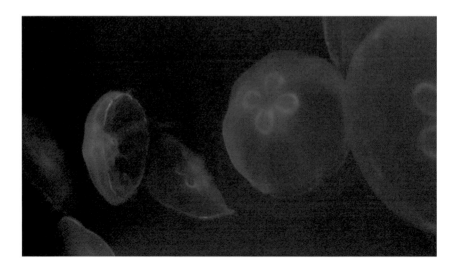

I know how he feels, sometimes I see how hugely I've changed over the 2 ½ years in which I've had therapy, since I realised how much I needed to change. At other times, it just seems so slow, or my mood might plummet and I feel like I'm back in a hopeless place. Unlike me snails must be very patient. (Anna: video diary)

My running shoes, I alternate them for each run. (Anna: video diary)

26. Snail/ 27. Running shoes

My hands. I trust my hands. My hands can draw. They can do anything. I've got great confidence in them. (Anna: video diary)

My feet. I've woken up feeling purposeless and fearful, trapped by worries. There's no particular reason, I'm sure. I've just tried to do a meditation my therapist told me about, in which the feet play a grounding role. I sat in my garden trying to imagine a very solid and reassuring connection to the earth through my wide, peasant-like feet. Feet like that ought to feel grounded, they were built for working in fields! (Anna: video diary)

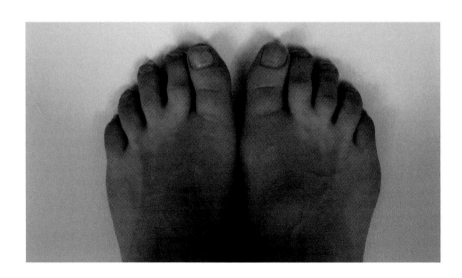

My gardening gloves, secateurs and two carrots I've just dug up. The sun came out and it was warm enough to garden. I feel so much better for spending the afternoon in the spring sun doing this. Now I've started on my garden I'll get into a routine watering and weeding it. I feel really happy right now. It's like my running – something I just get on with, without judging it. Gardening is good for me! (Anna: video diary)

30. Gardening gloves/ 31. Carrots

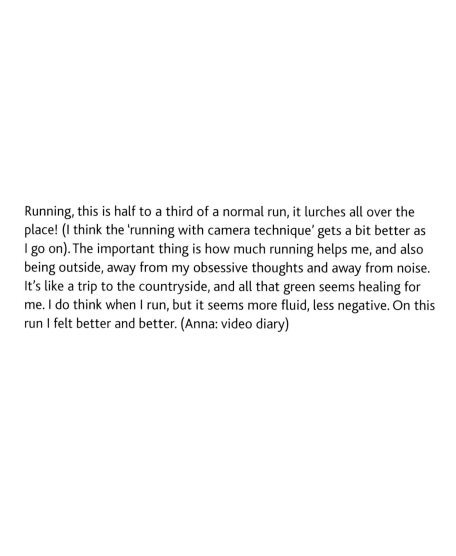

Running, this is half to a third of a normal run, it lurches all over the place! (I think the 'running with camera technique' gets a bit better as I go on). The important thing is how much running helps me, and also being outside, away from my obsessive thoughts and away from noise. It's like a trip to the countryside, and all that green seems healing for me. I do think when I run, but it seems more fluid, less negative. On this run I felt better and better. (Anna: video diary)

32. Running / 33. Lurching

This is the mail - I never pick up the mail, because it's a bit hard for me to bend down. I've explained to the neighbours that if it looks like somebody has just walked right over it, then that's exactly what's happened. It is an obstacle though. (Anya: video diary)

I think stairs are really beautiful. I always thought stairs were pretty great, ever since I was a little kid... Even now I see places that have got a spiral staircase in them, and I snap out of my usual attitude, which is oh fuck, a set of stairs, and think how beautiful they are. (Anya: video diary)

34. Post/ 35. Stairs

I usually like to start my day with some kind of physical activity. But that only usually happens if I have enough sleep. At the very least, I can do some sun salutations. … One book told me, every morning I should have room temperature water, with the juice of a fresh lemon, finished off with a pinch of cayenne pepper, which I don't have. I should drink all this before anything else. (Ava: video diary)

36. Sun salutations/ 37. Slicing a lemon

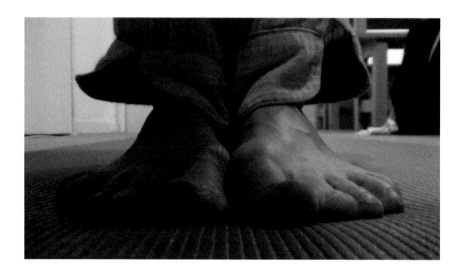

I love coffee, I love its flavour, its warmth, it's very comforting to me. There's something about the sound of a coffee maker, it just makes you feel like your day is off to a really good start! (Ava: video diary)

I'm really very careful about the way I call attention to my hands... sometimes I polish my nails, I like the way they look. (Ava: video diary)

38. Coffee brewing/ 39. Painting nails

I love walking so much, which is why I try to wear comfortable shoes. I really hate feeling restricted, to have my movement be slow because I'm tottering around in some shoes that are hurting my feet. At the same time, I really like to look stylish and I love fashion, and I do really love shoes. But because my arthritis has spread to my feet now, it's not really good to wear high heels. These were impractical in every single way, but when I saw them I really just could not resist! (Ava: video diary)

40. Comfy shoes/ 41. High heels

FOUR

Genes and organs

'Genes and organs' examines how the interiors of our bodies structure and influence our exterior surfaces and identities and shape our daily lives, and how the inner workings of our bodies, the circulations of blood and the flows of air, affect and betray us. Tracing the transmission of conditions from their interior origins within the body to the outside world and everyday life, this chapter considers how the inner landscapes of the body are both visible and significant.

The presence of illness drives the need to understand our bodies. When a part of our body no longer works or causes us pain, we seek answers to tell us why. But finding out what is wrong is not always a simple or straightforward process. Sometimes answers do not exist and when they do they do not necessarily provide a solution. This is especially true in the case of chronic illness, which often challenges medical expertise, can take years to correctly diagnose, and habitually defies treatment. As Ava describes, while "it's so easy for people to believe there's a solution for everything in a way, ok you're blind – well just get a dog and then everything will be ok; oh you're in a wheelchair – just start going to church, Jesus will save you" (Ava: interview), in reality we cannot always solve our problems or cure our bodies. But we can develop tactics for living with them.

We can, for example, learn the particular warning signals that our bodies send out. An asthma attack begins with a whistling, wheezy sound originating from Ami's chest, and a tight feeling in her shoulders. You can tell when her breathing is getting bad by the way her shoulders start to heave up and down as she struggles to get oxygen into her lungs. Her chest starts to feel hot and raw, and she can feel the pockets in her lungs fighting hard as they begin to close up. The lack of oxygen circulating in her body means that her teeth start to hurt and her head begins to ache. It gets worse and worse. Ami takes her inhaler, presses it, breathes it in, and hopes that in a minute the attack will subside. Up to this point Ami's actions follow a routine procedure. The wheezing is Ami's warning signal, telling her to watch out for asthma, to take care and to use her medication. Up to this point, the attack does not frighten her, because her body is telling her exactly what is happening inside. But if the inhaler does not dispel the wheezing as it should, the attack will continue, and it will get worse. This is the point at which asthma becomes frightening. All of a sudden Ami will feel weak, her chest and her head will start to hurt even more, her muscles, strained from the effort of trying to breathe, will begin to ache, and she will have to reach for the phone and call the emergency services. In this moment illness is transported from the safe interior of Ami's body to the outside world, transforming itself from a quietly sleeping beast to a life-threatening predator. Ami listens for these signals on a daily basis. She is equipped with a peak flow, with which she can measure her lung capacity, and with two different inhalers, two medications that she takes each morning, and four medications that she takes each night.

April knows that her epileptic seizures tend to happen in the evening. As a child, they only ever happened when she was asleep, when she did not know what was happening and could easily lose consciousness without realising, where there was no one to see or to help. They can last from a couple of minutes to three and a half hours, on and off, and are preceded by a ten second to five minute warning. The warning is what people classify as an 'aura'; it is different for everyone and no one else would be able to perceive the signal. In April's case, the aura is a slight loss of control of her arms; they start to snap, and then she feels dizzy and just knows that something is not right. When this happens, she has to lie on the ground. But once a seizure starts, that is it, she is committed for the long haul; it is a case of sitting through it because there is simply no way to stop it. Her arms stiffen, her head is thrown back, and she loses control of her body. There might be small breaks between moments of seizures, but there is no way of knowing how long the entire episode will last. It is exhausting, and the more tired April gets the harder it is to control. Perhaps the worst aspect of the seizures, worse than actually having the seizure itself and worse than the horrific bruises acquired as her flailing arms hit the walls or the ground, is the look of panic on the faces of those who witness this event. During this time, April can hear everything that is going on around her but is unable to speak, to tell anyone who is standing by it is ok and do not panic; there is nothing you can do. People close to her now understand and know what to do in this situation, but sometimes people will try to hold her down when she should not be restricted, or they will call an ambulance and she will end up spending the evening in the local accident and emergency department.

Learning these warning signals involves developing an awareness of the body, and a physiological understanding of how bodies work. Adrian's awareness of the muscular-skeletal structure of his body has changed in response to living with joint hypermobility syndrome, so that over time he has learned about muscle groups and how they interact; and Anya has tried to learn as much as she can about Miyoshi-type muscular dystrophy, so that she can understand what is happening to her body:

> 'I have to understand it as much as I can. It's a difficult thing to understand, without going and doing a lot more serious reading, I remember that at one point with my reading I had to open the medical dictionary at every other word. When you're trying to understand things on a molecular level it's impossible, it's impossible for me to understand that but it's important for me to try and understand what the condition actually is, and to get an idea of how much I don't know, if anything.' (Anya: interview)

Through the process of knowledge acquisition, we give attention to the body and identify and isolate the source of illness within it. Illness becomes attributed not to a failure of the body but to a single malfunctioning body part, a part that unlike the rest of the body is incapable of rejuvenation or repair:

> 'My pancreas – that's the main thing, that's the part of my body that's been sick. Because other things, they break, and they fix, they come back, you cut yourself and the skin heals back, but that is sick, it's not working, basically.' (Adam: interview)

By identifying a malfunctioning body part, the mechanism of dualism is brought to life. The body becomes re-known as a series of interconnected but distinct functioning and malfunctioning parts, and we learn the value of their individual functions, status and relations. Once a part has been isolated, we can attribute illness to the invader that feels like it has taken home inside us:

> 'I feel it's invaded my body. I don't resent my body; I resent the diabetes in my body. Yes, I do think it's very separate. I resent my pancreas a hell of a lot, it's obviously working in some way but it did fail me.' (Alice: interview)

The body becomes a fortress under attack, infiltrated by an illness that is in the body but not of it. The presence of the invader, the attack on one of our vital parts, forces the rest of the body to work harder, and the knowledge of what our bodies are coping with makes us more aware of their vulnerability:

> 'The one thing that has made me really aware of my body is the fact that one thing goes, one part of my pancreas goes, and everything else is fucked; you have to work twice as hard. There's an absurd statistic for diabetics about cigarettes, which is that for every cigarette a normal person smokes, that's like smoking five for a diabetic. Your body is constantly overworking.' (Alice: interview)

The shifting interconnections between this tripartite assemblage, made up of mind, body and illness, show how illness fragments the body. Illness is both within the body and separate from it, and, while it is always there, its presence fluctuates depending on how obvious it is at any given moment. This shift can depend on how we are physically feeling on a particular day, and it can be activated by our social relations and actions. The question, 'How is your arthritis?', for example, seems to identify Ava with her joints. Not seeing her rheumatologist for some time, in contrast, makes her feel distant from the arthritis.

Identifying and isolating illness within the body means that it is an invisible, hidden secret that can be kept private. Many conditions have no externally visible presence and those that do exist, such as bruises and injection marks, can be disguised or covered. This means that on a day-to-day basis no one needs to know, no one can tell, that illness is living inside our bodies. But illness is affective, and as it travels from its interior and invisible source into the outside world of everyday life, it becomes harder to hide and to separate from the rest of us. When meeting a friend for a coffee, Ava might let slip that she is feeling tired. This can easily backfire, as for example when her friend with a two-year-old daughter retorts, 'Why are you tired? You don't have a two-year old!' Similarly, a work colleague has started to think that she is a hypochondriac due to her frequent verbalisations of malaise. Ava understands that these mischaracterisations are not other people's fault; after all she has not explained the background or the context of her remarks, that feeling tired, run down and swollen are the symptoms of her condition and her everyday reality. At the same time, it never ceases to amaze her how people can assume that because she is young and single she should be out having fun, drinking and clubbing and staying up until four in the morning without feeling any the worse for wear the next day.

As illness moves beyond the body and is rendered visible, it affectively becomes a source of social stigma. Asthma inhalers and insulin injection pens stand out and announce the presence of illness. These material signifiers can be construed as signs of weakness and experienced as sources of embarrassment. As a child, Ami would wait until she was in a place where she could hide before taking her inhaler, suffering a little bit more in order to avoid the glances of others. Even without such obvious physical markers, the question of whether other people notice or can tell that illness is hiding inside us lingers:

> 'I wouldn't tell people. I haven't put myself in a situation where people would know … I just don't believe that people won't make assumptions … I might be kidding myself, maybe people do realise …' (Anna: interview)

> 'But I wonder whether people don't notice, I'm sure people must notice. There are times when it feels like it's this blaring siren on top of my head.' (Anya: interview)

Whether or not they can guess, there are times when we want to let people into our worlds, and to do this we need to tell them about our conditions. But telling people can be an issue; it can be hard to find the right time, people can be a bit standoffish, which is upsetting, and often they are shocked: because you look perfectly healthy from the outside they just do not expect it. You never can tell how others will respond or what assumptions they might make. Even doctors can make the wrong assumptions, reinforcing a negative stereotype of illness:

> 'I went to the doctor a few weeks ago with something completely physical, and it was a locum, I'd never seen him before. I think he must have flashed up my record and seen 'depressive episode', and all he talked about was, was I feeling ok, was I active, was I socialising, totally focusing on my mental health. It feels like a really dangerous label, a filter through which he's seeing me.' (Anna: interview)

Ultimately, it is not our bodies that take issue with illness; they can learn to live with the conditions that they face. But society places a high premium on the healthy, fully functioning body and singles ill bodies out as different, making them feel that they do not fit in:

'Do I want to get away from it? I want to get away from the things that make you very conscious of your body in society, but I love my body when I don't have to wear anything man-made, and by that I do include injection kits, and clothes, and all of that. I feel very comfortable with myself when nothing else is there. It's when everything else is there that I feel very aware of it; it doesn't fit in right, it's not quite there, I have to use things to make it do what I'm told it's meant to do.' (Alice: interview)

It is impossible to escape the fact that the public realm is a place reserved for healthy bodies, and that illness is deemed a wholly private matter. Alice's encounter on the bus perfectly illustrates the point:

As I sat trying to find a safe (technical term for bit of flesh you feel comfortable injecting) I got uncomfortably conscious of 2 separate people who sat beside me and behind me. The guy next to me was muttering to himself as he looked at his phone and the woman behind me had a very loud phlegmy cough. The man then answered a phone call from his 'sister'. He said 'yeah I'm alright, I'm on depression tablets ... gotta go and see one of those quacks that are on Lordship Lane. I'll take 'em but I'm not going.' At this point the woman's cough had got really loud and my instinctive thought about these 2 people and myself as I sat trying to inject and to block out the world was 'you bunch of freaks!' But then I realised it's not that the 3 of us are freaks, but that none of us were hiding our physiological conditions. It's not that as individuals we are freakish but that our confident acts of 'I'm injecting no matter what' and 'I'm "confessing" to depression no matter who hears' and 'I'm gonna cough because it really bloody hurts and I can't suppress it anyway' are freakishly uncommon in the public realm. Our bodies were public, something that is usually only reserved for a supposedly healthy physiology. (Alice: journal)

The significance of our internal bodies is exposed when it means that they resist being defined, categorised or typified by society. The discovery of gonads, which had previously been mistaken for ovaries, within Amara's body led to a life changing series of events. Things happened rapidly; within a few days of the discovery Amara was put under general anaesthesia and a gonad rectomy was carried out. The operation was performed laparoscopically; a tube with a video camera was inserted through Amara's navel to isolate the gonads and tiny one-centimetre incisions were made to take out the inactive material. Tissue that lies fallow in the body is the perfect place for cancer cells to start growing, so it was imperative that the gonads were removed from Amara's body.

Aside from having to come to terms with the fact that she is infertile – IVF and adoption are both possibilities – and getting used to her new body (because hitting puberty in your twenties takes a bit of getting used to) Amara has grown into a happy, healthy, woman. The HRT that she takes is easily mistakable for the contraceptive pill, something that is totally normal for a young woman to take. The scars from her operation have faded in time; they are miniscule in comparison to the six centimetre railroad appendix scar left from an emergency operation in a rural hospital in India when she was eight, a scar that has grown with her, becoming a three-dimensional thing with its own texture. But the surface of Amara's female body belies her internal biology, and Amara knows that being a woman is not quite as simple as it appears. Although she enjoys performing her newly discovered femininity – finding a different way of carrying herself, a different way of walking, buying new clothes and wearing makeup and high heels – the question that remains fundamental to her is, "I have XY chromosomes, and if everything went to 'plan' then I would have been a man. How do you feel about that?" (Amara: interview).

She cannot forget this question; it has been a defining aspect of her life. Conforming to society starts at an early age, and Amara had already decided that she was a woman and figured out what that meant, at least for her, before she found out that her biology was telling a different story. But she is also aware of the ways in which her biology has affected and will affect who she is, in different and telling ways, and there are still parts of her body that she does not understand, and that are changing beyond her control. She does not know, for example, what is going to happen to her body as she grows old. HRT does not just make Amara more feminine. Her body needs the hormones in order to maintain basic stability, to solidify her bones and to nourish her hair and skin. If she stopped taking her pills she would, in effect, become a post-menopausal woman – and these are the women her pills are designed for, women in their fifties who will only need to take the treatment for a few years to assist them as their bodies change. Because HRT is only intended for short usage Amara does not know how it will affect her in the long run; it is possible that she might age differently to other women, and that at some point she will have to stop the treatment. These questions and fears are captured on video in an intimate conversation between Amara and her boyfriend. Hidden behind a book, Amara's boyfriend uses a camera phone to look back at the video camera while she asks him a series of uncompromisingly honest questions:

> What do you think about my body?
> Do you think it's unusual?
> Do you think it's different?
> How do you feel about the fact that I'm intersex?
> Do you think you needed to know?
> How do you feel about the fact that I'm barren?
> (Amara: video diary)

These are questions that cannot be ignored.

The internal parts of the body, a fallow gonad, chromatic structure, failing pancreas, defective gene, narrowing bronchi or electrochemical impulse, each show us the significance of our biological foundations. Hidden inside the body they speak of the importance of invisibility; these are the private conditions of our lives, ours to keep secret if we wish. But as distinct and malfunctioning parts they also speak of fragmentation. Through their substantive failure they disrupt the interconnectedness of the body, allowing illness to affectively leak out of our bodies and into everyday life, and as our interiority flows outwards our bodies no longer seem natural or normal; instead we are made to feel socially out of place.

★★★

Other than during the induction of her first labour, April has been seizure-free since we last met. She takes medication twice a day and visits her consultant once a year for a review. Together, they are working towards reducing her medication to the lowest possible dose. She now has two young, healthy children. During her pregnancies, she had to be carefully monitored – her medication was increased to reduce the risk of seizures, and detailed scans to check foetal development were performed. The induction of her first baby at 40 weeks was stressful, triggering a seizure, but the baby was safely delivered by C-section. An elective C-section with her second baby avoided this dangerous situation a second time. As long as she takes her medication and takes care of herself, epilepsy is now something that April no longer needs to worry about, or think about too much.

Amara has moved to another country, and is finding that every doctor she speaks with has a different conception of how to live with the condition that she has – she is intersex. Her hormone regime has changed since we last met, when she was still taking high levels of oestrogen to help her body develop secondary sexual characteristics. After five years on this regime, it was time to reduce her hormonal intake and instead find the lowest dose at which her body could stabilise. Now, she uses a hormone patch, which means she no longer has to remember to take a pill every day:

> 'When they switched me to the patch I was a bit sceptical, because I swim twice a week, and showers, how is this patch going to work? You only change it twice a week, put it on on Sunday and change it on Wednesday or Thursday, and that's it. It was amazing in terms of not having to carry pills with you everywhere, and not having to remember to take a pill at the same time every day. The patch stays on; it's a much better way of delivering medicine because its continuous, which is what your body is doing as well when you're producing it in your glands, as opposed to eating a pill which means that you have a really high level for a few hours and then it drops, and this oscillating is not good for your body either. So I've been on the patch now for a year; it's so much easier.' (Amara: follow-up interview)

Unlike the pill, which leaves no visible mark, the patch leaves a little residue on her skin, a physical reminder of the last place Amara had oestrogen coming into her body. These marks wear away within a week or so, but at any given point there will be three or four of these left-over marks, usually on her midriff. Getting to this point was not straightforward: as her hormone dose was brought down Amara had to keep track of her body, taking note of any weight loss or gain, noting any increased hairiness. She met with a doctor every six months, each time discussing how her body was coping with the new level of oestrogen:

'It was weird because I don't know how my body is supposed to feel under normal circumstances. I think most of us don't consider what a baseline body is supposed to feel like. You only start to notice things when things are not feeling right. So, the lack of a negative response had to be the assumption of a positive result.' (Amara: follow-up interview)

At some point, Amara may need to stop using hormone replacement therapy (HRT) altogether. She has been thinking more about the long-term side effects of the treatment, and what it would mean to stop relying on medicine. Studies are starting to emerge on the effects of long-term HRT, but the treatment is still relatively new and it is something she needs to track alongside her own body. One way she has continued to do this, since taking part in this study, is by keeping a journal, noting her menstruation dates and any changes in her body. She also tries to meditate, and uses walking and yoga to connect with her body. The careful balancing act of maintaining just the right level of hormone is achieved through a mix of self-awareness and medical monitoring:

'I think we are so disconnected from our bodies and we're encouraged to think of ourselves as minds without bodies, and to acknowledge that our posture, our bodies have needs, and will affect the kinds of thoughts that you can have, that's very radical … you need to treat the body with the respect that it deserves and that means listening to it … I started meditating, and I'm really bad at that; it's really hard for me to sit quietly. It's easier for me to do a repetitive task, and thereby not think, so walking or yoga helps with being in touch with the body … And the other thing that's also very helpful is to do bone density tests, because that's a very nice way for medical science to tell you that your hormone levels are not right, because your bones are losing their density.' (Amara: follow-up interview)

Amara has also begun thinking about having children. She does not have any eggs, so it is not possible for her to get pregnant. But she does have a uterus, so with the donation of an egg and IVF it would be possible for her to carry a baby to full term and give birth. For the longest time, from when she was diagnosed until quite recently, she was sure that is what she would do, one day. Now that she and her partner are getting more serious about becoming parents, they have begun to consider other possibilities. She still wants to have children, but the couple are now thinking about adoption:

> 'I'm pretty much sold on the idea of adoption at this point. We've been to meet with an adoption agency … For me it's sad, but it's pretty final, there's none of this ambiguity. It would just be so much more bodily work, technological resources, and money that would have to go into this, and there are so many children that need adopting, it would just seem like a huge waste.' (Amara: follow-up interview)

FIVE

Feet and legs

Moving from the interior to the exterior, the book continues with 'Feet and legs', body parts that, as our connection to the earth and our way of navigating through the world, are perhaps our most direct link to the external landscapes in which we live. How do our feet and legs, as well as the shoes and canes that accompany them, connect us to, negotiate us through, and redefine how we know the built environment? How do our bodies redefine the topography of our worlds? This chapter considers the importance of these seemingly simple body parts and the influence that they have on the ways in which we move, dress and travel.

The revelation that she can be in touch with her feelings through her body really surprised Anna, because in some ways she has always tried to pretend that she does not really have a body. Now, when she is feeling anxious, floaty or groundless, she will allow herself to stop and catch her breath. Placing both feet on the ground, she can feel her feet being connected to the world, and it is just amazingly helpful to feel the solidity of this physical attachment. She will breathe deeply into her belly, calmly, counting her breaths, filling her belly up. And as she breathes she will try to feel how and where her anxiousness is manifesting in her body: the tightness in her chest, the trembling, her face turning red. She goes through each part of her body, identifying where the anxious feelings are located and pinpointing them. Then, when she knows each physiological expression of her emotion, she will imagine a stillness in her belly, so that the very centre of her being becomes a still, big, solid, safe place. As Anna slows her heart rate down and makes herself big and solid, she envisages her body as a vast landscape, a really big Antarctic wilderness or an Alpine mountain range, a place so big that nothing could undermine it, and in this way, she is able to establish a non-threatening connection to the world through her feet. Any bad feeling can be overcome using this technique that suspends the chain of thought, stopping thoughts from being piled onto emotions, and instead locating feelings in the body, where they can be felt and stilled:

> Second panic attack yesterday, I somehow 'caught' it; suddenly had an insightful view of myself and saw I was shaking & cold, nauseous, remembered to allow myself to

feel what was happening in my body. To place both my feet on the ground, breathe slowly, acknowledge this trembly, frightened feeling in my chest and gut, weakness in my hands. Then I visualised an immense landscape. Somewhere like the Alps or Antarctica, a place I always visualise when I remember to do this. The place is wild and uninhabited, somewhere I would feel safe from other people and where my anxieties are neutralised and scaled down. After doing this exercise (or meditation) I went into the meeting that had triggered these feelings. I felt completely calm and safe, nothing the people might say or do could harm me – it's as if the immense landscape is internalised, is actually me beyond my anxieties. (Anna: journal)

Slowing her breathing and grounding herself through her feet, Anna uses her physical connection to the world to help her cope with depression. For others, the felt connection to the world that feet provide plays the opposite role.

One way in which Ava is made aware of her condition is through her feet and her choice of footwear. In her video diary, Ava recorded two pairs of shoes – a comfortable pair of pumps and a beautiful pair of high heels – that evidence the constraints arthritis places on her love of walking and her love of fashion. The arthritis, which has spread from her hands to her knees and feet, means that wearing comfortable shoes is important. But, while she tries to be nice to her feet and not squeeze them into shoes that are uncomfortable or that hurt, sometimes she cannot resist the attraction of a pair of high heels. Shoes are just one item of apparel among many that can become signifiers of the presence of illness, compromising our choices and tastes through the unwelcome social signals that they send out. Ava's father once bought her a magnetic bracelet, which was supposed to get rid of pain when she wore it:

And I wore it for a few times, but it wasn't that attractive and I felt I had to draw the line somewhere, although I'm into alternative medicine and believe anything could work really. I just felt funny wearing it, as if everyone who saw me wearing it knew that I was wearing it to get rid of pain…
(Ava: video diary)

Having to regularly inject into her legs has left a mark on Alice's body. Injection sites leave visible lumps and bruises, and she now feels uncomfortable wearing summer clothes that will reveal these marks of illness: "I've got lumpy legs from it; I can't stand summer because I'm so aware of it, if I go into the sea or something, here are my bruises" (Alice: interview).

Having diabetes creates practical, as well as emotional, relationships with clothing. Alice has to carefully consider what to wear before she goes out on any given day. The need to inject throughout the day means that she needs to be able to access her leg or stomach, and the question of whether there is a way of injecting with any decorum is one that she often faces. While it is possible to inject directly through clothing, doing so is not advised as fibres can enter the body. It took Alice five years to stop feeling uncomfortable and conscious about injecting in public places. If she's wearing a dress or a skirt she might be able position the fabric like a pair of shorts, but if that's not possible then she'll have to search out a toilet to provide some privacy:

> 'The only thing now is, like today, I'm wearing a dress and it can be a bit difficult, having to find a loo can be quite frustrating. There's always an element, like it's a bit scummy having to do it in the toilet.' (Alice: interview)

Injecting insulin is a daily event for Alice and she recorded it in her video diary, the video camera zooming in on the needle piercing the skin of her stomach. Filmed in silence, the moment purposefully lays bare the reality of living with type 1 diabetes, and challenges the viewer to look when they would normally turn away. The footage has the power to show that injecting insulin is a discreet, clean and domestic act but at the same time it can evoke reactions that re-perform Alice's own experiences of injecting in public, as she explained during her interview:

> 'The points where I have felt uncomfortable have been at work once, where a woman, she was an idiot, she was frustrating in every possible way and it made so much sense when she said, "Do you have to do that here?" I was injecting at the lunch table, which she wasn't eating at I should point out. We got into this whole debate, about well would you do that to a type 2 diabetic taking their tablet. When you inject it's very discreet really, it's into the belly, and quite frankly my attitude is that if someone doesn't like it then look the fuck away, because I can't look away, I have to put it in my body. But the best bit was when I

said, "But it's not like I'm injecting heroin!", and she said, "Well really what's the difference?" Where do I begin with that?' (Alice: interview)

The injection kit, which is contained within a small black case, has become another material fragment of Alice's everyday life. More domesticated object than medical instrument, it is always with her, both physically and emotionally:

'The injection pens that you use are amazingly, you know, they look like a pen and the needle's tiny, I mean it's smaller than your finger tip, so I feel that it's a very domesticated thing and I do feel like the pens and my blood test, I keep them with me, there's an element of ... however small it is, psychologically it's a lot bigger than a little purse. It's a very frustrating thing. I feel attached to it, I have to know where it is; I don't leave the house with it – ever. These things are always, always on my person.' (Alice: interview)

The attachment that Alice feels to the kit demonstrates the significance of this small object, which has in a sense replaced the function of her pancreas. Her body, and her life, is dependent on it. The kit is always close to her, not a part of her body but a part of illness, an ever-present reminder of the dependence and fragility of her body.

Muscular dystrophy is slowly taking Anya's legs away from her. At the age of thirty-one, she has now lost most of the muscles in both her legs, including her gastrocnemius, the anterior of her lower legs and her quadriceps. Each time she loses a bit of her body, Anya has to find another bit to take over. The worry is that the more the disease affects her body the fewer bits there will be left to compensate. When she first started losing her calf muscle she fell quite a lot. These are the really scary moments, when she does not know if her body is going to find a way around the latest loss or not. But once she got used to not having the muscle in her calf she found that there were other strong muscles in her legs that could take over. Now Anya can still walk, even though the condition has taken out her quadriceps, which means that putting weight into a bent knee is impossible. She uses her core strength and each time searches to find the adjustments that will work, making gradual changes to the way that she moves and finding ways to get around the problem. It is doubtful that, if somebody who had normal legs suddenly had Anya's legs, they would be able to walk at all; it would be like learning to walk all over again with prosthetic legs, because essentially that is what they are now: "My legs really are like prosthetics, in a way, not to insult them or anything, but in terms of how I use them" (Anya: interview).

Making Polaroids with Anya resulted in a series of three prints that gave a 360-degree perspective of her legs: front, side and back. While I had asked Anya if I might photograph her legs, it was Anya who suggested the prints be taken from each angle. Looking at the resulting images together, she told me that they were exactly like the ones on her medical chart. While I was initially taken aback by what my methods might be recreating, Anya explained that the objective knowledge of her body held within the chart was comforting to her – who and what those images were for was concrete and reassuring. Without having made the prints together, I would not have had this insight into the way in which Anya, her body and medicine interrelate. In her interview, we had only spoken about the frustrations, anxiety and fear that have defined her experiences in hospitals and with the medical profession. Here was an instance that highlighted both the comfort of medical knowledge and Anya's ability to hold onto her own body in medical settings. The encounter turned notions of the medical gaze on its head.

Naked, as they were in the Polaroids, it is easy to see that Anya's legs have wasted away. But it is hard to say how apparent Anya's condition is to the outside world. She is young, attractive and fit, but she also walks awkwardly, has incredibly thin legs (even when clothed) and uses a cane. The cane itself is an elegant specimen of blond maple wood with charred stripes, nothing glamorous but a solid and essential companion. The idiocies of the well-meaning but insensible, the romantically inclined and the just plain rude have included enquiries as to whether there is a reason for it and asking whether the cane is a fashion statement. Even neighbours who do know Anya can be ridiculously inconsiderate, chaining their bikes to the handrail and making it impossible for her to negotiate the two steps down and one step up into her flat. The camera wobbles as she records this entrance on video; she needs both hands for the step and is forced to walk right over the mail, which lies scattered across the doormat.

The inconsideration of individuals is however matched, if not exceeded, by the kindness of strangers. Last year Anya went through a phase of falling a lot. In fact, she got to a point where she would catch a cab somewhere, get out, and hit the pavement. Falling itself happens so suddenly that it is hard to know what has happened: caught at the wrong angle her ankle will collapse and she will fall like a puppet, hitting the ground hard and fast. People who witness this might think that she has had a heart attack, because it simply does not make any sense, it does not fit into anything that anyone is used to seeing. But each time she fell there was someone there instantly, offering to help, offering to call an ambulance and trying to assist her back up to her feet. This is no mean feat, because with no leg strength Anya cannot use a helping hand to pull herself up. Further panicking and confusion will ensue from both Anya and the unsuspecting stranger as she attempts to explain her condition, that she is not trying to be brave, that she really just cannot get up that way, before she finally manages to lift herself up using her hands, with her legs carefully balanced underneath her and using whatever solid object is available nearby to her advantage.

The soles of our feet and our legs are the starting points with which we relate to the broader environments in which we live. The surfaces of the body bring us into contact with the surfaces of the world, highlighting points of connection and of disjunction in our everyday lives. Through the individual needs and restrictions of our bodies we develop particular relations to the environment. In Anya's case this means that she has developed an intimate knowledge of her local neighbourhood and how to navigate through it:

> It's my everyday reality; how can I safely get about the place and maintain my independence, my sanity, and all the rest of it. I know my environment in great detail and how to move through it; with new things, I make an educated guess and I never take stupid risks. So, if I've found a way better than a wheelchair, I believe I deserve respect for the amount of strategic thought that involves, as well as the accomplishment of staying out of one. (Anya: journal)

Anya knows exactly where places are, where to get coffee or a sandwich, and how far they are from the other places she needs to be. It can be hard to eat on the move, and if she thinks it is going to be a problem then she will eat at home before going out or wait until she gets home again. She uses the same strategy with transport. She knows the distances, the obstacles, how tired she is likely to be and when. And if she gets tired, then she has to make do with the closest option. For Anya, these measures are a way of living independently. But other people, family and friends, can get frustrated that she moves slowly, or with the limitations of how far she can go and where she needs to stop. They have suggested that it would be easier if she were in a wheelchair. This suggestion highlights the tension between Anya's body and social expectations of it. Once again, the problem of illness is transported beyond the physical boundaries of the body.

There are many things for Anya to watch out for in the streets: uneven, narrow pavements, prams and their militant drivers. Everyone else in the street moves too fast, and it is not obvious to them that Anya might fall if they touch her only slightly:

> I walk carefully, slowly. A few weeks ago, as I slowly and carefully crossed at a zebra crossing, the men in the waiting car furiously honked at me and yelled at me from the windows. The man in the passenger seat had such an ugly face. Sometimes I don't go out because it has become too frightening and too much hard work dealing with people – asking for a seat, asking people to move, needing help up off the pavement. (Anya: journal)

It would be easy not to try, which is one way of dealing with it. Anya is able to work from home and can do her grocery shopping online, so there is not that much need to leave the environment that works for her. Sometimes she cannot be bothered to walk down the hill from her flat to her local shops, not because it is difficult, but because it will take so long. The daily interactions with people that she faces when she does go out do not make it any more appealing. The man furiously honking his horn at the pedestrian crossing or the people on the bus who do not think to give up their seats make the outside world an ugly place:

> 'Some people can take one look at somebody with a cane and just know that hills and stairs are or could be a problem, and other people, I don't know what they think canes are for, I don't know what they think is going on. It's like people who don't give their seats to old ladies, things like that, what do they think is going on there? They've just got no concept.' (Anya: interview)

In her video diary, Anya contemplates the staircase that leads from her flat down to a communal garden. The camera peers down the steep metal staircase, issuing a sense of vertigo. The stairs lead down to a small concrete landing and into the back garden of Anya's flat, which is laid to lawn. A sense of stillness permeates the screen, then the camera suddenly zooms across the garden to track a city fox trotting by, getting lost for a moment in the greenery then finding focus again on a garden table and chairs which lie fallen on the grass, before returning to rest on the staircase. Anya is talking, but the noise of a helicopter passing by above interrupts and forces her to pause for a moment. The drone seems to fill the screen as she waits. She swings the camera left to the garden next door, taking in a sideways shot of a staircase like her own. Stairs pose a problem for Anya, and she rarely risks the descent into the garden:

> Stairs are a big problem; there are stairs everywhere you go, that's how most people manage buildings. But they're a real part of me negotiating whether I can go places. Sometimes I can manage stairs well enough on my own, I've been feeling pretty fit lately. I'd probably make more of an effort with these stairs if it wasn't so bloody cold, and in any case, there's this bit down the bottom, down there you can see there's a bit of a landing and there's nothing for me to hold onto to get onto the grass, and even with my stick it's a bit tricky to get down into the yard … This is also the way that I have to think about how I get about every day, how I'm going to get there, get inside, get myself out, especially on my own. If my partner is with me and we're travelling or whatever, there's always the unexpected flights of stairs and hills and things that are hard to manage, and we hire cars or, well, we've hired a car before, and he carries me up the stairs, which is lovely, and we manage that way. But obviously, it can get a bit tricky … I think stairs are really beautiful. I always thought stairs were pretty great, ever since I was a little kid. I grew up in an area where it was pretty flat, and we never had stairs in our houses when I was a kid, except for the house when we lived in the Northern Territory, all the houses there were on stilts, for cyclone reasons. But most of the houses in Western Australia, all the other houses I lived in, they didn't have stairs. So when I was tiny I used to get really excited by stairs. And of course, even now I see places that have got a spiral staircase in them, and I snap out of my usual attitude, which is oh fuck, a set of stairs, and think how beautiful they are, how nice they are. (Anya: video diary)

Anya's attention to the politics of priority seating on public transport is shared by others who also depend on their feet and legs to move through public space. These seats highlight the ignorance of society, but they also symbolise disability. When Aiden's arthritis is aggravated, especially if it is in his feet, knees or hips, he would love to be able to sit down on the tube. But he would be too embarrassed not to give up his seat to the people who more obviously, more visibly, need priority seats:

> Sometimes when things are aggravated with my A. especially if it's in my hips and/or feet and/or knees I'd love to sit down, but I'd be too embarrassed not to give up my seat to the obvious people needing the priority seats. The day I don't give up my seat, or even worse, take the seat off another, is when I'll feel as though I've lost. (Aiden: journal)

Despite the fact that getting on a crowded tube is likely to strain his arm or pull it in the wrong direction, so that pain cuts through and he loses his grip and falls, and that he always notices his knees going down the escalators to the tube, morning and evening, he will not give in. Being out in public spaces means that Aiden is at risk of getting caught out by his arthritis. His knees can give in on a simple shopping trip or his foot might start hurting out of nowhere and cause him to limp. It is embarrassing to be limping down the street, and, more importantly, there is that nagging fear asking how long it will last. But, as Aiden writes in his journal: 'This is the competition between me and my A. Not going to be a grandpa just yet – not 'till I've got kids and they've got kids' (Aiden: journal).

For Adrian, it is the very need to sit on the daily commute to work that causes his body problems. The journey, which he recorded in his journal and video diary, begins with a cycle to the train station:

> So, its 6 o'clock on a weekday morning, and I thought I'd give you a sense of going to work. So, probably very dangerously, but it's very early and there's no traffic, this is me cycling to my train station, all good fun. So, my train journey is about half an hour into Marylebone station, and then I have a little walk to Baker Street station, and then I take the underground for a few stops from there. A very strange sort of mixed up journey which always seems to hurt me. But then again, what's the alternative, maybe I should just give up my job and live in a swimming pool,

but then I'd need to win the lottery. Bit of a steep slope here, so I think I'd better switch off. (Adrian: video diary)

After a short, five-minute cycle, he boards his train:

6.04am Get on my usual train on my usual carriage; commuter heaven or hell, depending how you look at it. 6.04am is v. early but at least you always get a double seat … The problem, though, is the complete inability to design a seat that one might wish to sit in for half an hour, twice a day, 200+ days a year. You have two choices. Choice 1 is to slouch. This is prima facie more comfortable, but you pay the price ultimately. Well, I do anyway. The pressure required on my legs to support my weight, subtle as that is, is sufficient to cause a throbbing in my hips/glute muscles which then lasts much of the rest of the day. So that's not much good. Until I consider option 2, which has been recommended by my physio, which involves supporting yourself with no backrest. Much better posturally, but before long it makes my mid-back ache like mad. Option 3 (rarely used) is to stand. I do sometimes, but not often.
6.39am Arrive at station, walk to Tube station. Good to get some walking in the morning, although the shoes I wear make a big difference to comfort levels. The combination of plastic orthoses and smart leather office shoes makes my back judder with each step. Not always noticeable, but when I stop to think about it, it feels like it's not helping when I walk. As a result, I tend to wear (where I can get away with it) trainers/pumps; a little like women wearing trainers instead of heels to commute, only a little less dramatic a change.
7.07 Arrive in office to usual morning routine. (Adrian: journal)

Airports and aeroplanes all cause similar problems for Adrian, making getting about in the world a difficult and painful process. Airport chairs rarely offer back support, and travelling on business trips involves lots of walking in uncomfortable smart shoes. It does not get any better once he has boarded the plane:

Now time for my 6am flight to Zurich. Only 90 mins, and I fall asleep, but the damage is done. It is, frankly, impossible

for me to sit on an aeroplane seat in comfort. They force
you to slouch, basically. Sometimes I sit cross legged (yes,
correct!) on plane seats with shoes off. I'm small enough
to do it. I get odd looks but I don't care if it helps ease the
discomfort. Looking a bit odd comes with the territory.
Maybe I'm a bit eccentric anyway, but I will often stand
and stretch my back, legs, neck, wherever I happen to be,
especially when travelling. (Adrian: journal)

Other, simple and mundane everyday discomforts include sitting on
a park bench or a wooden chair. At home in the kitchen Adrian has
a cushion on his chair for comfort. He admires how his children can
sit on anything with perfectly pain-free backs; he was like that once.

Moving, walking and sitting, bodies encounter obstacles and
negotiate their own ways through the world. The material fabric of
everyday life seems to be designed in order to put bodies on display.
Social space engenders the public consumption of bodies and conspires
against their material flesh, changing the topography of our worlds
by making our bodies feel materially, as well as socially, out of place.
Plastic orthoses, injection kits and canes draw attention to the material
discomfort of our being in the world. These objects highlight the needs
and the deficits of our bodies, which are dependent on them. But they
also show how, through constant adaptation, we compose new ways of
being. By keeping these objects close to our bodies and incorporating
them into our everyday lives, we form new partnerships that help us
to overcome the presence of illness and allow us to navigate new ways
through the world.

★★★

Alice is married, and lives with her husband in a small rented flat in
London. She is now on an insulin pump, a new technology that has
changed her relationship with diabetes. The pump is a portable device
(a little larger than a pack of cards), attached to the body via a catheter
placed under the skin of her belly. It continuously delivers amounts
of rapid or short acting insulin to her body, giving Alice increased
ability to control her blood glucose levels. Making the switch to this
new way of living was not easy - it was like being diagnosed all over

again, and took time to adjust to. Finding the right cannula (the tube that is inserted into her body) took several years, and left her with sore and bruised skin. The type she is on now is similar to the insulin pen needles that she used to use, and can be left in her body for no more than forty-eight hours. This new routine is a challenge:

> 'It added a whole new level to my routine, because you have to be so much cleaner with your skin and you have to be careful with the pump, and I'm messy and clumsy and all of those things.' (Alice: follow-up interview)

It has also been difficult learning anew how to calculate the dosage she needs, and because it is fast acting Alice has found that her sugar levels have been spikey:

> 'Diabetes always needs an incredible level of self-management, and it formalises that in terms of the amount of maths – so much more. It's crazy because you're now having to work with insulin sensitivities and base rates and bonus rates and what they're feeding at and whether that ratio is changing...' (Alice: follow-up interview)

The pump itself dangles from her body, a little virtual pancreas clipped on inside her clothing but prone to falling off and getting caught on door handles. Despite these difficulties, Alice does not feel that she could return to her old insulin injections now; she is committed to living with this new device.

Adrian's condition, joint hypermobility syndrome, remains the same – just as it has since it first affected him:

> 'I don't feel any different now in many ways to when I was twenty-one. It is what it is, I've got no sense that I expect anything to worsen.' (Adrian: follow-up interview)

Despite this stability, the last seven years have been eventful. A specialist gave Adrian a new, additional diagnosis of fibromyalgia (FM). FM is a condition characterised by chronic, widespread pain, which typically responds to pressure. Other symptoms include fatigue. But FM is hard to diagnose, and the medical profession varies on whether they choose to accept it as a valid condition. Adrian did his own research, joining FM organisations and reading up on the condition, but he is still not entirely sure that the diagnosis is correct:

'What was difficult is it wasn't actually clear that's what I had; it fitted up to a point, it explained the fact that I have this constant low-level headache throughout my body, but it didn't fit so clearly within the classic mould. I had no issue when it came to energy levels, and that's one of the main things that sufferers get. A doctor had given me a diagnosis, but I'm still not actually convinced that it's right.' (Adrian: follow-up interview)

In the time since we last met, Adrian has also tried new treatments to ameliorate his pain. He has tried injections and private prescriptions, but the drug-based regimes did next to nothing to help. A welcome break from work, between jobs, meant that he could spend more time running, and he found that not working at a desk, moving more and getting more sleep all helped, a little. Adrian's children have also grown, and no longer need picking up or carrying around, relieving his body of that extra strain. Having searched for answers and spent considerable amounts of money trying to relieve the pain that he experiences on a daily basis, Adrian has now reached a point of acceptance:

'I haven't been pursing it, and I haven't felt the need to push, I've had various aches and pains and injuries, but I haven't felt the need to pursue it. I don't know if that's a good thing or a bad thing, but that's the ways it's worked out. There was a period of time when I was, if you like, on a mission.' (Adrian: follow-up interview)

SIX

Hands and hearts

In the video diaries made for this study, hands feature more than any other body part. Fingers point out bruises, apply medications and toy with pills, nails are painted and objects are held. Holding more significance than their physical presence first suggests, hands perform acts of care, enclose pain and symbolise strength, and in this final chapter they speak of the interconnections between mind, body and world. 'Hands and hearts' considers the emotional connections between bodies, minds and landscapes, and touches on themes of finding a home and belonging in the world. Through this chapter we see how, just as illness refuses to be contained within bodies, bodies refuse to be confined by illness.

Anna trusts her hands. Focusing on her hands in her video diary, she shows her confidence in them to the video camera. Her hands can draw and play musical instruments, they are sensitive to textures, and they are strong and flexible. She does not have any of the same doubts about her hands that she does about her mind and its thoughts. She never thinks twice about their ability to do things, and they do not seem to suffer from anxiety or self-hatred. She imagines that if her mind were as reliable as her hands then things would have been a lot easier. Unlike her mind, Anna's hands just get on with things, without worry or doubt. Her thumbs are even a source of comfort and self-assurance, something to hold onto when she is feeling anxious. Like her feet, Anna's hands provide her with a sense of her material presence in the world. They are symbolic of her whole body, which stands in polarity with her mind. But this does not mean that her body is unshakeable. There are days when Anna feels like she has no skeleton to hold her together, days when she feels like a jelly that will wobble any time someone sneezes or breathes heavily around her. It can feel like even light criticism will demolish her, like a badly built house in strong wind. On these days, her sense of not being good enough is expressed in her body's shakiness and tiredness. This visceral anxiety, a shift of bad feelings from her mind to her body, hints at a connection between the two. It is not simply that Anna's mind is weak and her body strong. Depression runs through her entire being, affecting both mind and body. But there is a difference between these two parts of herself, and the difference is trust. When Anna's thoughts drive her around and around in circles and drive her to delusions, she knows that her mind is being destructive and unhelpful; that it is getting her into trouble. But when her body throws her into the state of panic, it is not lying to her or trying to trick her. Instead, it is telling her something she needs to know. So Anna has come to rely on all her physicality to save her, and, she knows that her body has the power to transport her away from depression.

In her video diary Anna also recorded a short clip of a ruined old house, for which she wrote the accompanying note:

> The point is it looks how I feel, or rather how I felt yesterday, like a horrible old house with grumpy monsters inside it bashing their heads against the walls. The monsters are responsible for the ruined state of the house, as I feel I've somehow chosen to be like this – if only I could make better choices, do things more constructively, if only I really wanted to be happy I could be. I feel cross with myself for making things like this. (Anna: video diary)

On the days when she feels like this she knows that she can get out of her real house and go onto the common. Looking at the trees and the distant places, the external things that are bigger than her, things that are solid and immune to ruminations, the bad feelings evaporate. Faced with the immensity of the landscape, whether a real London park or an imagined Antarctica, anxieties become scaled down, neutralised, unreal. Depression has influenced Anna's life in every way, and that is probably the most depressing thing about it. It has held her back and restricted what she has felt able to do, and her constant checking on what she is feeling, managing her emotions and monitoring her body, is a form of training that she imagines is a fairly contrived process. But learning to live with depression has also brought a new, positive connection to her body: now, she feels that it is her body that can help her, on a good day. Some things it has taken away and some things it has given her, and other things remain to be reclaimed. Yet despite all the ways of being in her body that Anna relies on, she still feels an extreme mind–body divide in which her mind has precedence. Anna has been socialised to deny her body; that view has been a big part of her background and it is something that continues to be enforced by contemporary culture. So while Anna knows that it is problematic to think of the mind and the body as two distinct things, and that not everybody in every culture feels that distinct separation, she cannot get away from that way of looking at things: she is separate. More than anything, she aspires to not feel that split. But it is almost like she can feel where the perimeters of this territory are, it is just so clear: the barbed wire and the guard post.

Adam remembers the sensation of the skin covering his hands drying out and cracking as his body, attacked by diabetes, suddenly lost the hydration and nutrients that it needs to maintain elasticity. It was one of the first signs that something was really wrong. Now, his hands are marked by little pinpricks, tiny little dots, which last for a couple of days and then are gone, before new ones quickly appear to replace them. When he gets in the shower or the bath and he looks at his fingers that are made vulnerable by the water, he can see all the holes. Adam has to check his sugar levels by pricking his fingers. He's been pricking the final third of his finger for four years now, and the skin is starting to thicken out a bit, so he has to search a bit harder to find a little soft spot. These marked hands and the memory contained within them are a reminder of illness. The toughening of the skin in response to the routine of injecting is a private and intimate mark that can be felt but hardly seen.

Ava's hands also embody her condition, and she films them in her video diary. Some days she is extremely aware of her fingers that feel big and fat and unfeminine to her. While arthritis has spread to other parts of her body now, her feet, knees, and her neck, her hands remain the most significantly affected. These were the place where arthritis first manifested and presented itself, and they are how she continues to monitor its progress:

> I spend a lot of time thinking about my hands, but also, I spend a lot of time looking at them, down at the keyboard … A while ago I wrote a piece for a writing contest, sponsored by the arthritis society, about my experience. And it's about a woman I knew, who lived next door to us as a child, and I called it 'Hands', just because I tend to think about my own a lot. (Ava: video diary)

Ava continues, reading her piece to the video camera out loud:

> The symptoms started ten years ago; I was twenty at the time. Skin stretched and burned red to accommodate the swelling of my finger joints. Blood seemed to pool in my hands. I walked with slightly clenched fists to alleviate the feeling. I thought this is what it must feel

like to trek through the tropics on a diet of too much salt.
(Ava: video diary)

Ava's hands are an ever-present symbol of illness, connecting her to
her past and to her future. A photograph of her mother reveals an
uncanny family resemblance: matching pairs of hands that appear
identically swollen. But Ava's mother does not have arthritis. And
the childhood memory of seeing an old woman's rigid, curled and
frozen fingers has imprinted itself on her, as though it knew its own
significance was to come years later. Ava's hands seem to haunt her. It
is not that the arthritis incapacitates her, or that it is painful, but that
it is always present. It is always there in her hands, making her bodily
awareness acute and insisting that she listen to her body. She continues
reading out loud:

> I've been disabused of the notion that one can control
> everything, that our human minds can outwit our human
> bodies. But I know now my body will always do what it
> wants, I can only try not to provoke it. I can only be kind.
> And listen, as attentively as I would to a child … Despite
> these physical changes, it's my relationship to time that
> has changed the most. None of us are promised things
> will unfold as we wish, yet taking note of the small yet
> discernible shifts in my body has made me more aware of
> the small and discernible shifts everywhere. My body, with
> its hypersensitive antennae, is always responding, making
> me take note not just to it, but to the life around me.
> (Ava: video diary)

During one of our meetings I asked Ava if I could photograph her
hands, the site of her illness. Agreeing, she positioned them on the table
in front of me, nails neatly polished in a femme fatale dark red, fingers
spread. We chatted as I prepared the camera, the Polaroid instamatic that
I had specifically chosen because of its ability to reproduce fragments
of the flesh in an immediate and tactile format. During the two or
three minutes while I photographed, Ava rearranged her hands several
times. Together with the frustrations of painful fingers that lack the
dexterity they once possessed comes a careful attention and care, from
her choice of rings – she's very careful about the way in which she calls
attention to her hands, and anything that makes her fingers look big
or swollen will be rejected – to the match between her skin tone and
the colour of her nail varnish. These hands, which she thinks about

a lot, are both a site of illness and of normality, a delicate balance between femininity and betrayal. And while they moved on the table in front of me, they always returned to the original position: palms down, fingers spread. Because this is how Ava's hands are normally inspected: by the x-ray machine, which monitors the progression of the arthritis within her joints.

Beyond the physical reaches of our fingertips, our hearts beat not with illness but with the vitality of life. Our bodies tell us of their presence, but they also tell us of the presence of life. They tune our attention to the details of our material being, to the environments we inhabit, and to the small and ordinary things in everyday life. Alice's body leads her; if it feels tired then she cannot ignore it, she must really listen to what it is doing. It can make her appear a bit wishy-washy or moany about things, and it can sometimes make her seem like quite an ill person. But during the moments when she feels like not bothering or giving up, her body has other ideas. It tells her that she is not allowed to ignore it, that she has got to continue and do what it needs her to do, so that she can stay alive. Since the age of fifteen she has been aware of the fact that at some point she is going to be vulnerable, at some point she is going to die, and she holds dear this fact. It has made her conscious of what she is going to do with her life, what is important to her, and what can make her happy.

For Alice, the dynamic between mind and body sometimes seems like a battle between two opposed forces. Anna tangibly feels the split. But other examples make clear how, in the end, mind and body cannot be separated. Aiden describes his mind and body as good friends. For almost ten years he has been asking his body 'why?' when he's getting off the bus or walking to the tube and one of his joints protests. He is in constant dialogue with his right shoulder, the most affected area, and a part of his body that he uses every single day. They do not always agree, but the shoulder always wins, and the more it wins the less they disagree. The arthritis is a personality in itself, a constant entity that he is catering for and carrying with him, that he is always trying to establish a good dialogue with and trying not to hurt. As soon as he is not mindful of his body it becomes vocal in making him mindful of it. In his video diary, Aiden captures an intimate moment between him and his shoulder as his fingers apply a medicated rub and he explains the actions that triggered the pain. For Aiden, mind and body are symbiotic. Having arthritis does not define him and it does not destroy his life; it just means that he has to do things differently, like a tall person has to duck when they walk through a door, and a short person has to stand on a stool to use a top cupboard. Being tall or short does not make a person's life unliveable or not as good as an average sized person; it simply means that they negotiate the world differently.

Depression is not specifically located in Amelia's head; it is not even necessarily there at all. Her mind can feel like it is too full of stuff, but the parts of her body that are in pain when she feels depressed – not a physical pain, but a feeling of badness – are her stomach and her heart. The feeling in her stomach is akin to the bad effects of not eating and sleeping well, while the pain in her heart is a heavy, constricted feeling that sits across her chest, different from the sort of sadness that can make your heart ache. The interconnectedness of head, torso and stomach make it hard for Amelia to separate out her mind from her body, they have such a large impact on each other. But the experience of depression as a whole has made Amelia more aware of her body. When she is not feeling very good she will try to ignore it, because it bothers her that she has had an impact on it, and vice versa, when her body is feeling better she enjoys her awareness of it. It follows that when Amelia is feeling good her body feels more like a part of her, and when she is feeling bad it feels less a part of her, something she regards from afar. Because of these experiences, Amelia continues to feel quite negatively about her body. There is a certain seriousness about how she has felt in her body that continues to occupy her mind.

Adrian's pain shifts around his body, seeking the path of least resistance: through the entire length of his spine from his lower back to his neck, extending down towards his shoulders or up into his head. It moves fast; fifteen minutes ago, he had a throbbing sensation just off to the right-hand side of his lower back, a low, dull ache in his right hip, and a little bit of a tingling sensation just off to the left-hand side of the C6 joint in his neck. Now, most of the back pain is gone and the pain he is experiencing in his hip has doubled. But regardless of where it is, the pain is always present, constantly moving but never leaving. It is a low-level, headache sensation, and it consumes whatever available mental bandwidth it can so that at any point in time a certain amount of Adrian's mental capacity is absorbed by the fact that he is hurting. When he is engrossed in something his consciousness can push the pain to one side, so working hard is good, but conversely when his brain is less active the pain will rush in. Adrian's body is shouting at him, all the time. But there isn't much that he can actually do about it; there is nothing that will materially change the fact of the matter. So instead of listening to his body he tries to concentrate hard on other things, and in doing so he can take his mind away from the pain. There is no doubt an element of mind over matter in living a life of daily pain.

Minds and bodies find their own routes through everyday life, flowing and fluctuating between interconnection and separation in their efforts to live. Their relations are often defined by their immediate conditions, but they also speak of a connection to landscapes and their belonging in the world. Anna has built up a solid relationship with her immediate local environment over time, and photos and drawings of large, blossoming trees featured in her journal. They are trees that she has been photographing and drawing for nearly twenty-five years. She runs past them several times a week, and simply looking at them feels beneficial. Ami's garden is a place that gives her a sense of accomplishment and peace. The tomatoes, chilies and flowers that she grows show her that with care life can flourish. Aiden's rheumatologist warned him that his psoriasis, which made his mouth dry, left him constantly thirsty, and covered his hands in paper-like cuts that cracked and made the skin split, would get worse in London where the climate is so much dryer than his home in city in Australia. In fact, the condition has almost entirely disappeared during the five years that he has been living here. Amara feels that she can never live in a remote village cut off from civilisation, because every six months she needs blood tests to check her hormone levels are correct, and every twenty-eight days she has to visit the doctor to get a new prescription. She has to make a special case if she is travelling for any length of time. Apart from the necessity for careful monitoring, no more than a six-month supply can ever be obtained because the hormones in the pills are active and have a very short validity; after six months they will expire, becoming useless. Once, in the humidity of her southern Indian home, all those pills melted, the sugar coating attracting ants. Up until a certain point, Anya's life seemed to be defined by Australia's beaches. She grew up strong, swimming and body surfing at every free moment, aware of the powerful ocean. Her likes and dislikes were determined by her physicality and she was immersed in a landscape of bush walking and ocean swimming. Now she wonders if she can face going back to that landscape. Before she left two and half years ago, she could no longer get down to the beach and into that ocean unassisted, and the long hot summers were excruciating. The physicality of Australia's landscape creates differences between people, and perhaps going home now would be like shoving a square peg into a round hole. England's landscape, by contrast, could be a chance for Anya to continue redefining what she loves about life.

For Anya, the idea of returning home to relive a life is now lost; her body no longer fits into the landscape of her childhood. What this tells us is that, if to be home is to belong, then where home is must be defined not only by where we have come from but also by where we fit in. The conditions of belonging exist in our histories and memories, in our social relationships and environments, and in our material bodies.

★★★

Aside from the transition to an insulin pump, Alice has been through some difficult times since we last met. She has lived through two serious family health scares, and been diagnosed with depression, which has added to her 'wibbly wobbly' feeling:

> 'What's been really striking about the whole transition from 2009 to now has been understanding my body and the fact that my diabetes is always going to be wibbly wobbly because your body is always wibbly wobbly, and basically, I was diagnosed with depression in 2010 and from then through to now have had bouts of it … When it hit again in 2014, I remember saying to my husband that I just thought I'd grow out of it, that it was just something that would pass, and he said, well maybe it's more that you're growing into it, and it's something that you will live with. Kind of like the diabetes I guess.' (Alice: follow-up interview)

Yoga, gardening, and walking all help with both her diabetes and her depression, giving Alice a routine and supporting her mood. She is, as her husband said, continually learning to live with her body and growing into her life.

For Anna, life has made an upward turn. She is now fifty-one, and feeling much more positive about life. A death in her family brought her closer to her siblings, and a new partner (something she did not think was ever going to happen in her life) has given her new connections to the world. A new therapist, too, has helped her develop techniques for overcoming her anxiety and feel more connected to her body. She now feels more in touch with herself and more in touch with other people, and as a result she is no longer isolated by her depression:

'I've done a lot of work since then … One of my problems was that I was not hugely in touch with my body, not hugely grounded, the legacy of a traumatic childhood. I think it's really helped me to be in touch with what I'm feeling and to break through loops that weren't getting me anywhere before. Things have improved hugely … I slowly became better at trusting other people, enjoying the company of other people, valuing how other people break your isolation … I think there's more acceptance in a way, I'm much kinder to myself, more forgiving of what I might have seen as my weaknesses before.' (Anna: follow-up interview)

One new technique involves 'reality checking' – Anna reminds herself where she is, that she's grown up, that she knows how to be okay. She looks at things in the room, counting how many flowers there are in a vase or how many shoes on a shoe rack, something that gets her back to now and stops her wandering off in her head, a wispy state that keeps anxiety going. This focused technique helps to ground Anna, and reassures her. Exercise is still important, but she is less driven than before, gentler. She had reached a point where she was running ten miles a day and could not bear to be at home, but now she is spending more time gardening instead of running. Still, she always tries to do a certain number of steps a day. Generally, her sleep is better too, although she still has to focus on her breathing to ensure that she does not wander off into new thoughts at night. Her routine is slightly less predictable than before, partly because of work and partly because having a partner, someone else, changes that rhythm:

'I can't cling to routine – predictable routines were so important to me, but that's changed now … I'm not as routine-bound. But there are other routines, my partner has got two dogs and walking them is part of our daily life. There are smaller routines. But I'm not as trapped by routine as I was.' (Anna: follow-up interview)

Conclusion

Learning from the lives portrayed, this conclusion seeks to relate some of the findings in the book to other literatures and ways of thinking about illness in more detail, providing some evidence for the arguments that the book makes and offering a more theoretical discussion. As Les Back (2015: 821) writes, researching everyday life 'makes us take the mundane seriously and ask what is at stake in our daily encounters with neighbours or the people we brush past at the bus stop'. This chapter explores what is at stake in these accounts, from ideas of care, control and choice, to bodily doubt and the felt politics of stigma. While the study draws on only twelve accounts, it is worth remembering that around 15 million people in England have a long-term condition (including around 30% of the population under fifty) (Department of Health, 2012). This conclusion discusses the bleed between private lives and public issues, showing how personal lives and modern life are intimately entangled and highlighting the relevance of these accounts to contemporary society.

Rhythm

The first three chapters in this book considered how eating, exercising and sleeping are unique sets of material practices, through which the significance of the body becomes evident and lives are woven together. All bodies need nutrition, exertion and rest; these needs are so fundamental that we usually take them for granted. But the rhythms of eating, exercising and sleeping reveal and hide the presence of illness, showing us that bodies are both vulnerable and strong. For Henri Lefebvre and Catherine Régulier, repetition and habit have always been essential characteristics of the everyday. They point out that modern life is modelled on 'abstract, quantitative time, the time of watches and clocks' (Lefebvre and Régulier, 2014: 82). With our lives running on abstract time, from the hours of sleep and waking, to mealtimes, work and private life, we force our bodies to fit a rhythm that is not their own. Lefebvre and Régulier (2014: 84) suggest that this model of time sooner or later gives rise to the dispossession of the body, so that 'He who rises at six in the morning because he is rhythmed in this way by his work is perhaps still sleepy and in need of sleep'. In illness, as we have seen, abstract time becomes harder to keep to, it is painful or even dangerous to ignore basic needs, and it becomes apparent that bodies need to run on their own time.

Less flexible than healthy bodies, ill bodies cannot bend to social rhythms without breaking. They demand a particular predictability and structure to the day. They need a routine, an interval of time to eat, or more time to sleep. These are things that all bodies need, but illness makes them more apparent, and significant. Ava's morning routine, which begins with several sun salutations and ends with a healthy breakfast, keeps her busy for an hour every day. This means that she cannot simply roll out of bed, and leave the house. Routines like Ava's can become rituals of care, but they are hard to keep and structure is not always desired – it can make bodies feel dependent and regimented. Illness and the apathy that can accompany it, which makes managing time difficult, can also drive people to ignore their bodies and deny their needs. When the preventative measures that are taken are not always effective, the temptation to ignore the body is easy to understand. It is hard to accept that we do not have complete control over our bodies, and continuously looking for cause and effect patterns, answers, and solutions when there may not be any is ultimately frustrating. As such, rhythms can reveal the shifting nature of illness, from presence to absence, and acceptance to denial. But denial is no resting place – a long list threatens those who do not take care or keep good control. Blindness, kidney failure or heart attack all pose the risk of a more certain outcome for the body.

In *24/7: Late Capitalism and the Ends of Sleep*, Jonathan Crary argues that our rhythms have shifted over time, showing that there has been an alarming shrinkage of sleep in modernity. Almost any 21st century city might claim to be a city that never sleeps, round-the-clock work and consumption have disrupted the night, and rest is becoming incompatible with modern life. As Crary (2014: 17) writes, '24/7 steadily undermines distinctions between day and night, between light and dark, and between action and repose'. The conclusion is that, 'within the globalist neoliberal paradigm, sleeping is for losers' (Crary, 2014: 14). This attitude resonates with Ava and Aiden, who recognise their own need for sleep as being greater than the average and out of step with the tempo of modern life. But the corrosion of sleep is not simply a personal trouble, it is also a public issue – after all, we are all getting less sleep:

> Over the course of the twentieth century there were steady inroads made against the time of sleep – the average North American adult now sleeps approximately six and a half hours a night, an erosion from eight hours a generation

ago, and (hard as it is to believe) down from ten hours in the early twentieth century. (Crary, 2014: 11)

Cut loose from notions of necessity or nature, sleep is becoming an increasingly urgent social problem. While many of us may continue to function on the modern norm, others are beginning to suffer. The need for sleep, recognised by ill bodies as a vital part of life, should be taken as a warning bell for society. The neglect, dismissal and devaluation of sleep in our restless times shows that sleep is not simply an issue of self-governance, it is also a product of contemporary capitalist society – it is both personal and political. As Crary (2014: 25) writes, 'As the most private, most vulnerable state common to all, sleep is crucially dependent on society in order to be sustained'. Sleep is a basic human right, and is fast becoming a source of inequality.

It is important to recognise that sleep is not simply dormancy. As Ava and Aiden show, sleep is a productive capacity, and rest can be a better cure than any drug. In *How to Sleep: The Art, Biology and Culture of Unconsciousness* Matthew Fuller (2018: 48) writes that 'Sleep is stirred into illness in uneven ways'. While sleep can be an act of care, there are other times when sleep becomes a problem, as Alice and Anna's video diaries showed. Hypos and insomnia can interrupt the night, making it hard to rest or feel rested the next day. This 'sleep debt' (Fuller, 2018: 135), loss, or deprivation, can easily accrue, taking its toll on the body and everyday life. Finally, the meanings, methods, motives and management of sleep (Williams, 2005: 1) are varied, showing that there is an art to sleeping well (Fuller, 2018: 6).

The contemporary compression of time, our lack of sleep at night, is also felt during the day. It can be hard to find the time to prepare a meal, or to exercise regularly. As a society, we are becoming less active, more sedentary. People in the UK are around 20% less active now than in the 1960s. Outdoor activities are being replaced by time spent working at a computer, on the road or watching TV. We are at a point where we need to make a conscious decision to build physical activity into our daily lives. This is true for all bodies, but it is critical for bodies that are more vulnerable. It is not simply a case of being more active, but also of spending more time outside. As Richard Louv writes, research has shown that 'green exercise' is more beneficial than going to the gym:

Researchers in England and Sweden have found that joggers who exercise in a natural green setting with trees, foliage, and landscape views feel more restored, and less anxious, angry, and depressed than people who burn the same amount of calories in gyms or other built settings. (Louv, 2010: 49)

Anna's experience of running outside illustrates this point – as she noted for her video diary, 'all this green seems healing for me'.

The speeding up of life also leaves less time for cooking. The contemporary assumption that we do not need to spend time preparing food, that fast food and ready meals make cooking efficient and convenient, leaving more time for other activities – the idea that 'the increased speed of fast food facilitates life' (Abrahamsson, 2014: 293) – works against bodies that need to eat in particular ways. While we are all encouraged to eat five portions of fruit and vegetables a day by the national '5 a Day' campaign (following a recommendation by the World Health Organization), as part of a healthy, balanced diet, it is hard to eat well without dedicating time to shop for and prepare food. There are social and structural problems that interfere with eating well too – the marketing strategies of the food industry, supermarket layouts and social inequality all impact on our eating habits (Vogel and Mol, 2014: 315).

From the speed of cooking and eating, to the speed of food in the body – the speed with which food is broken down and absorbed – food, and the speed of food, can be a problem for ill bodies. Alice carefully weighs out her portions, making sure she consumes just the right amount, and selects food options that help her body by limiting the amount of sugars and carbohydrates that she eats. Anya chooses foods that will nourish her body, and that she can easily digest. Ava takes time to prepare her food, enjoying the rituals of care that go into shopping for the right ingredients. Rebalancing the importance of food against other activities, the participants in this study show that food can be a comfort and a cure. As Sebastian Abrahamsson (2014: 288) writes, 'Food produces rhythms, patterns, and temporalities, punctuating everyday life through practices of cooking, eating, and digestion'.

The idea that contemporary life is characterised by increasing speeds is a concern voiced by many. Thinking about the speed of life draws attention to social norms and expectations, and entails rethinking what sleeping well, exercising well and eating well might mean. While there is a history of resistance hidden within the everyday, there is also a tendency for the everyday to reshape itself:

> Even though, at various points in history, the everyday
> has been the terrain from which forms of opposition and
> resistance may have come, it is also in the nature of the
> everyday to adapt and reshape itself, often submissively,
> in response to what erupts or intrudes in it. (Crary, 2014:
> 69-70)

The submissive nature of the everyday, its tendency to adapt to larger
social pressures and forces, combined with the tendency within our
society to address bodies as passive objects of knowledge or treatment
decisions, means that it is difficult for bodies to make their own
choices and follow their own particular routines. But the accounts in
this book speak of and against the social organisation of everyday life,
highlighting the conflicts between the body and society. In grasping the
measure of its own rhythms, the living body is made present, animated
by its own score. The body serves us as a metronome (Lefebvre, 2014:
29). Marking the beats of life, it becomes a constant reference point
through which we can learn a symphony of rhythms, with each organ,
function or part of the body having its own rhythm to be heard. As
Aiden wrote in his journal:

> I'm generally quite aware of my A. and how it affects my
> body but since receiving this journal and not knowing
> what to write about, I've paid a little more attention to my
> joints. My shoulders seem to have a little rhythm of their
> own. My right shoulder will be the main source of pain/
> uncomfortable till about 15:00 and then it'll swap with the
> left shoulder. (Aiden: journal)

Listening to their own bodies, the participants in this study show
how it is possible to learn the body's needs and its limitations, and to
care for it. Listening entails making choices, learning to refuse social
demands, and finding other ways of living, but it also creates the
possibility of choosing to ignore the body's own instructions, even if
there are consequences to pay. In these instances, the importance of
embracing life is made clear.

Finally, it is worth remembering that we cannot maintain a constant
state of attentiveness, and that our experiences of illness come and go,
marking out a different kind of rhythm. As Anya wrote in her journal:

> I've been thinking that there are some stories I could be
> telling but that I'm not. There are times when I feel that the

daily peculiarities of my illness, its chronic-ness, dominate my life to the extent that everything else seems to hinge upon them. It's like walking around with a gaping wound. Then everything calms down, or you force it to so that it doesn't make you mad and/or bitter and so you can get on with things without the drama. In the calm periods, I don't want to relate those things so much because A) I'm calmer and I don't need to so much, B) I'm calmer and they seem boring, C) They seem boring because they're the same things happening over and over, D) I'm afraid that if I talk about them I'll get worked up all over again and tie myself up in knots of frustration. (Anya: journal)

Care

While eating, exercising and sleeping can become acts of care, at other times they are used as forms of control. In *The Logic of Care*, Annemarie Mol writes that it is impossible to control diseased bodies – they remain unpredictable and erratic. Instead, 'The art of care … is to act without seeking to control' (Mol, 2008: 28). Her study, based on conversations in hospital consulting rooms, shows how care is an ongoing process, a question of tinkering and fine-tuning: 'Caring, or so it appears, is a matter of attuning to, respecting, nourishing and even enjoying mortal bodies' (Mol, 2008: 12). She also points out that in scholarly discussions about health care, 'care' is often distinguished from 'cure', marking out the difference between daily activities such as washing, feeding or dressing wounds from interventions in the course of the disease that hold the possibility of healing. In her book, she avoids making this distinction, suggesting that for people living with long-term conditions the activities categorised as 'care' and 'cure' may instead overlap:

(Caring) food and (curing) drugs may have similar effects on a body. Caringly dressing a wound may help its cure. What is more, nowadays many of the diseases that send people to their doctors are chronic in character. A so-called cure of such conditions does not lead to recovery but instead makes life more bearable: it is a form of care. Thus, even if the interventions in the lives and bodies of people with chronic diseases are often knowledge-intensive and technology-dependent, there are good reasons for calling them care. (Mol, 2008: 1)

This definition of care resonates with the accounts in this book, and can be seen in the ongoing practices of care (and cure) that are described through the rhythms and routines of everyday lives. While caring for bodies can be tiring, frustrating and saddening, caring practices also illuminate the positive relationships that we build. Being ill gives us a reason to pay attention to our bodies and to protect them, providing the justification we need to do simple things, like spending money on a massage or taking extra time in the shower. Instead of seeing illness as the body letting us down, responsibility is transferred and we invest ourselves in being healthy so that we will not let our bodies down:

> 'Yes, sometimes I think, actually I'm probably so much healthier now that I have this, because it gives you permission to look after yourself. And, for some reason looking after yourself, it seems so simple but it's so hard, and not just the logistics of it but mentally accepting that. I think it's taught me a lot too about taking responsibility, because, I think, you know it's so easy to wish that somebody will come and take care of you, and that you can just abdicate responsibility for yourself, and it's so easy to get caught up in those fantasies I think, no matter how independent you are, but this is something that has finally made me say, ok I have to take responsibility for myself.' (Ava: interview)

Ava's comment draws attention to the difference between being cared for by another, and the self-caring practices that this book has focused on. Ultimately, there is both a sadness and a joy in this awareness.

Practices of self-care also draw attention to the taken-for-granted tension between health and pleasure. In a study of dieting in The Netherlands, Else Vogel and Annemarie Mol question this dichotomy. Observing alternative dieting advice, they suggest that healthy eating might not require people to control themselves and abstain from pleasure. The study juxtaposes self-control with self-care, showing how cultivating bodily pleasures can train the body to make healthy food choices. Shifting controlling behaviour and the thought 'am I being good?' to self-caringly enjoying food and the thought 'is it good for me?', it becomes possible to feel what the body needs, and to enjoy (just the right amount of) food. Vogel and Mol show that self-care involves cultivating an attentiveness to the body, but they also recognise that 'While rules seem to offer a stable kind of control, there is no end to the tinkering self-care that involves feeling' (Vogel and Mol, 2014: 311). As they note, there is a thin line between liberating the body and imposing obligations to care (Vogel and Mol, 2014: 315). These ways of thinking about the eating body are also explored in the accounts of eating in this book, which show how care and pleasure become tangled up in the act of living.

In/visibility

The next three chapters in this book illuminated the sheer physicality of our being in the world, revealing how illness flows through the material spaces of our bodies and lives, reshaping the details of everyday life at every scale. From internal fragmentation to external placelessness, the interiors of our bodies and their external surfaces act as spatial registers of illness, creating points of disjunction between body, mind, illness and world. We try to keep illness hidden inside the closed spaces of our bodies, disconnected from the outside world, and we learn to recognise the signals that it sends out from within so that we can calm it. But despite our best efforts illness sometimes refuses to be contained. It affectively leaks out of our bodies and announces its presence to the world. At other times, the world challenges our bodies from the outside, revealing and reinforcing their deficits and their vulnerability. As Monica Fraser and Mariam Greco (2005: 27) write, the material fabric of everyday life seems to be designed in order to put bodies on display.

One way in which illness is made visible is through the things we wear. In a study of footwear, identity and transition, Jenny Hockey, Rachel Dilley, Victoria Robinson and Alexandra Sherlock (2014) explore how the temporal landscape of shoes interrupts the life course, showing that past and future identities can be returned to or avoided through our choice of footwear. To put it simply, shoes make things visible. The stigma of shoes and the need to value comfort over fashion, a choice usually reserved for later life, is made apparent by Ava and Adrian, who are careful to avoid impractical or painful shoes. By prioritising comfort, Ava and Adrian accelerate their future age-based identities, highlighting 'the 'work' achieved by objects that share an owner's spatial journey' (Hockey et al, 2014: 259) and showing how shoes can make illness visible. Aiden writes in his journal: 'My feet are really sore at the moment. I blame it on crap £5 plimsoll shoes; no cushion from impact of walking' (Aiden: journal).

Illness is made visible in other ways too. In his classic study *Stigma*, Erving Goffman (1963: 9) defines stigma as 'the situation of the individual who is disqualified from full social acceptance'. There is little to repair or add to Goffman's conceptual scheme, but it is possible to illustrate the concept of stigma with examples from this book. In particular, Goffman's distinction between the 'discredited' and the 'discreditable' plays out in these pages. The discredited person assumes that their stigma is perceptible or evident to others, while the discreditable person assumes that it is not (Goffman, 1963: 14). This in/visibility seeps through everyday life, exposing people when they are in social situations or public places, and forcing them to continuously consider how much 'social information' they might be, or might want to be, conveying about themselves (Goffman, 1963: 10). Alice's journal entry illustrates how as a society we usually keep our troubles private. Trying to inject insulin on the bus, while overhearing a 'private' phone conversation and sitting near a coughing passenger she wrote: 'Our bodies were public, something that is usually only reserved for a supposedly healthy physiology'. Anya finds herself questioning other people's perceptions of her walking stick, and her condition, bringing to life the displeasure that Goffman describes:

> he is likely to feel that to be present among normal nakedly exposes him to invasions of privacy, experienced most pointedly perhaps when children simply stare at him. This displeasure in being exposed can be increased by the conversations strangers may feel free to strike up with him, conversations in which they express what he takes to be morbid curiosity about his condition, or in which they proffer help that he does not need or want. (Goffman, 1963: 27–28)

Anya's own experiences, of being stared at by children and questioned by adults, are recorded in her journal:

> At Pilates one of the instructors has a little son who asked his mother, why does that lady have a walking stick? … Perhaps she didn't want to speak about something she thought might offend me. Children asking about it does not offend me. (Anya: journal)

The presence of the stick, her slow pace, the constant risk of falling, all expose Anya, making her condition public. April feels this too – a seizure in public is a tale of embarrassing exposure, as Goffman describes: she 'may regain consciousness to find that [she] had been lying on a public street, incontinent, moaning, and jerking convulsively – a discrediting of sanity that is eased only slightly by [her] not being conscious during the time of the episode' (Goffman, 1963: 106). Other conditions are less visible. Arthritis makes Ava feel swollen and tired, manifesting itself in her fingers, hands and feet, and sometimes in her knees. But hidden beneath the surface the condition is invisible to the eye, affording some protection from the otherwise public consumption of her body. She finds herself in the position of the 'discreditable':

> The issue is not that of managing tension generated during social contacts, but rather that of managing information about his failing. To display or not to display; to tell or not to tell; to let on or not to let on; to lie or not to lie; and in each case, to whom, how, when, and where. (Goffman, 1963: 57)

Her efforts to conceal her arthritis can cause Ava to display other weaknesses, or to miscommunicate how she is feeling. For example, when meeting a friend (who does not know about her arthritis) she might say she is tired, and be rebuked by her friend – after all, her friend might think, why should she be tired? Aiden writes in his journal:

> Lying in bed after numerous 'snoozes' I'm thinking if I was ill, like with a cold or gastro or whatever I could call work and say I'm not well enough to come in, but I can't (or is it won't) call to say my A. won't allow me to get to work. I could say I'd be late but then people stop depending on you – you get put in the faulty basket.
> At least with the flu people are cautious not to catch it from you. But everyone at work knows you can't catch my A. Therefore there's no benefit for them with me taking time off.
> Knackered… (Aiden: journal)

All of this means that unthinking routines can become management problems, as Goffman (1963: 110) writes, 'The person with a secret failing, then, must be alive to the social situation as a scanner of possibilities, and is therefore likely to be alienated from the simpler world in which those around him apparently dwell'.

While Goffman focuses on negative experiences of stigma, there is (sometimes) another side to these encounters, which can be seen in the kindness of strangers. Julie Brownlie and Simon Anderson (2017) write that small acts of kindness are part of how we can open our imagination to the lives of others and understand city living. Different from civility or politeness, the less expected quality of kindness 'involves low-level, unobligated, interpersonal acts and relationships which have direct practical but also affective or atmospheric consequences that are subtly transformative of the relationships in which they occur' (Brownlie and Anderson, 2017: 1228). Small acts of everyday help and support include sharing food or accommodation, delivering a paper, taking a parcel in, or simply saying hello. These 'ordinary' interactions are hidden in plain sight: 'There is a paradox here: at some level, kindness involves an awareness of others; yet it often occurs at so low a level that it is barely visible, even to those directly involved' (Brownlie and Anderson, 2017: 1225). Ordinary kindnesses within the accounts in this book include strangers offering help after a fall, and a housemate setting up a coffee maker.

As Brownlie and Anderson (2017: 1229) recognise, kindness is not an unquestionable good: 'even "good" acts can have dark or unintended outcomes, including affective risks. Because of the risks linked to being dependent, for example, we can come to feel "undone" by kindness'. Illness can also be misunderstood, making other people's acts of kindness frustrating, and recognition can be embarrassing, uncomfortable, obtrusive and intrusive, making it hard to know how, or if, to react or respond to the in/visibility of illness.

Belonging

Attending to the spatiality of the body shows how bodies are made to feel dysfunctional, out of place, and lost in the world, both socially and materially. But moving through the body and following the movements of the body through space also reveals something else. Just as these spatial scales fragment and disconnect us, they also create points of connection, turning our attention to our bodies and our lives, and heightening our awareness of our corporeality and mortality. Using the materiality of the world in partnership with our material bodies, we are able to adapt to the conditions of our lives and find new ways of being in the world. Space illuminates a series of fluctuations: between visibility and invisibility, stability and instability, and placelessness and belonging. It shows how, through various activities, we change and manage our boundaries. There are instances when our bodies are confronted by the world, times when we feel alienated – from our bodies and from the world – and moments when we feel connected to and through our embodiment and environment. Our bodies are ours to hold onto, and the ways that we live in them and through them on a daily basis remind us of what is at stake. Just as illness refuses to be contained within bodies, bodies refuse to be confined by illness. They are a vital force, and, ultimately, they urge us to embrace life.

Havi Carel (2013) describes how in illness 'bodily doubt' – loss of continuity, loss of transparency and loss of faith in the body – replaces the bodily certainty that characterises normal everyday embodied experience. The year before we met, Anya went through a period of falling. Her bodily doubt led her to stop going out: it had become too frightening and too much hard work dealing with people – asking for a seat, asking people to move, needing help up off the pavement. The world around us can shrink, and the body can be reimagined as a fortress or a prison. It can protect us from the world and it can isolate us from it, it can hold us captive, and its walls can crumble around us. Jean Améry (1994) describes how, as we age, the body shifts from being our mediator in the world to become our prison:

> This body, which is no longer the mediator between the world and us, but cuts us off from world and space with its heavy breathing, painful legs, and the arthritically plagued articulation of our bones, is becoming our prison, but also our last shelter. It is becoming what remains, a shell. (Améry, 1994: 35)

Ultimately, our bodies are our final resting place, and our feelings towards them speak of the ways in which we truly inhabit the world. Just as our hands are in all our actions and thoughts, our bodies are our homes, because, while they do not always provide us with peace, shelter and stability, in the end home is, quite literally, where the heart is.

Appendix: Sensuous scholarship

As C. Wright Mills (1959: 195) writes in 'On Intellectual Craftsmanship', his own appendix to *The Sociological Imagination*, sociology is the practice of a craft. This appendix offers some craft lessons, describing how the study that this book is based on was made, and recounting some illustrative fieldwork tales. The subtitle to this appendix is borrowed from Paul Stoller's book, *Sensuous Scholarship*, in which he challenges the idea that the body should be considered primarily as a text that can be read and analysed, and argues for the importance of understanding the sensuous epistemologies of the body. Expanding the sociologist's standard repertoire of methods, the study in this book combined interviews with video diaries, journals, drawings and photographs, disrupting usual ways of telling and extending the 'range, texture and quality of what passes as academic representational practice and writing' (Back, 2013: 28). These visual methods also evoke other senses and feelings, including bodily 'smells, tastes, textures, and pains' (Stoller, 1997: xiv). By using these methods, I hoped to make an intimate, textured and sensuous account of living with illness – one that would not reduce bodies to 'lifeless texts' (Stoller, 1997: xv).

Over the year of my fieldwork I gradually recruited participants through online adverts, email lists and personal contacts. Participation in the study was open to anyone living in London, aged between eighteen and fifty with a long-term physical or mental health condition. These parameters were set to avoid logistical issues involved in working outside of the city and to exclude issues specific to childhood and ageing. I met with everyone who contacted me, eventually stopping when I felt that the sample consisted of an adequate gender mix, some social class diversity, people at various life stages, and a range of conditions. After an initial meeting to discuss what participation in the study would involve, I interviewed participants and, as part of the interview, asked them to complete hand-drawn questionnaires. These meetings were designed to be intimate, taking place at home or in familiar public places. Each participant then had the choice of making a video diary and/or keeping a journal. We later met again so that I could collect the video camera and journal and discuss any issues and concerns, including how I intended to use the material that I had been given. After scanning the pages of the journals and copying the video footage that had been recorded I returned the original journals and DVDs of the unedited video footage to the participants by post. This appendix focuses on the paper journals and video diaries, outlining how they were made and discussing the vivid and vital encounters, observations and data that they produced.

Journals

While the interviews had focused on biographical and medical histories, at the end of this meeting participants were given journals in which to record day-to-day life, which they were asked to keep for one month. This time period was flexible and some journals were kept for much longer. The idea was to extend the period of data collection, and the life of the study, without making it too demanding (diaries have been kept for research purposes for much longer periods of time, up to and over a year - Bartlett and Milligan, 2015: 38). As Ruth Bartlett and Christine Milligan (2015: 8) write: 'Being able to gather data for a longer period of time is important when seeking to understand the daily rhythms of life, or if you wish to study changes within a person, such as coping strategies'.

Each journal had a brightly coloured hard cover and squared graph pages, providing a format that invited drawings as well as words. A5 in size, they were small enough to be kept close and carried around, and entries were made on buses, tubes and trains, at home, at work and on holiday. These qualities helped to differentiate the journals from the medical diaries that several of the participants also had to keep, or had kept in the past. Medical diaries are intended to record neutral facts, to score pain and to monitor diet, and the participants who had kept them reported finding the task frustrating to the point that their records were often incomplete or abandoned. It was important that these journals invited a different kind of engagement. They came with a short and simple set of instructions, providing a starting point for how to use the journal, without being too prescriptive:

> Please keep your journal for one month, it is up to you how frequently you write/draw in it during this time. The idea is to make an inventory of the things that are important to you and the things that happen to you in relation to your body and your condition. As well as writing, I would like you to make lists and to count things. This might include a list of the medications that you use, a list of words that describe your body, or counting the number of times something related to your condition happens in a week. I would also like you to make a day survey – choose one day and write about it in detail. (Instruction sheet)

The idea to write lists, to create an inventory of everyday life, was inspired by Georges Perec's love of list making (2008). Perec is a playful and inventive master of classification, and he revels in making lists. I hoped that the invitation to write lists would help the participants begin their journals, and that the task of list making might be less daunting than writing a long entry on a blank page. List making is also, as Perec shows, a wonderful way of documenting the 'infra-ordinary' – the things we do every day. These details of day-to-day life often fall out of interview accounts, in part because participants fail to recall them retrospectively, but also because they may not seem important in an interview situation. Everyday life is not a typical feature of narratives or medical histories, which focus on significant moments such as diagnosis, treatment and monitoring. Nor is it something that people often choose to discuss with friends or family, either because the condition is kept private or because they do not want to complain about it too often to others. As Margarethe Kusenbach writes:

> Ethnographic interviews can miss out on those themes that do not lend themselves to narrative accounting, such as the pre-reflective knowledge and practices of the body, or the most trivial details of day-to-day environmental experience. (Kusenbach, 2003: 462)

Diaries, in contrast, are noted for their value in recording everyday routines and practices. One of the advantages of the diary method is that participants can record events and feelings spontaneously and as they occur, gathered in the moment. As such, they are the perfect method for attending to everyday, small stories and experiential, day-to-day worlds.

While everyone understands the idea of a diary, the participants used their journals in different ways. Some wrote lists, others wrote longer entries, and some participants deviated from the focus of the study, using their journal in a more personal way. As Ruth Bartlett and Christine Milligan (2015: 41) write, 'there can be considerable variation in the length of entry and the degree of personal revelations a person will enter into the diary'. While most of the entries were written, from a few lines to a few pages, some of the journals also included drawings, as well as other found objects – postcards and tickets – inserted between the pages. These intimate records, memoirs and logs came together in rich and compelling personal accounts. The journals were used to record daily observations, social encounters, patterns of behaviour, personal thoughts and memories, offering small insights into everyday lives and highlighting otherwise taken-for-granted details. As Ava wrote:

> So maybe this journal will be a collection of not just my own feelings and thoughts about my own body, but about all of those random anecdotes I overhear and don't know what to do with. Because there is a societal idea of the body and one's very own idea of their own body. (Ava: journal)

Not all of the participants were motivated to keep a journal – Amelia, for example, found that it was another task that she had failed to complete, while Adrian decided to type his journal, finding it easier to make notes on the computer. For Alice, keeping a medical diary was a task that needed to be completed but which she resisted. The fact that this activity was situated outside of a medical context, where there was a different motivation and a different reader or audience, meant that keeping a journal was a task that could be fulfilled on more personal terms and which allowed her to make her own health intervention:

> 'What I really need to do, and having a diary will be useful – especially a nice moleskine because the DAPHNE one, it's just not the same, it's NHS, it's a bit orange and a bit white and a bit wrong – but I need to write it down day-by-day precisely what I'm eating, precisely where my sugar levels are going, that would really help, I know that will help.' (Alice: interview)

And later:

> Curiously (or maybe not really) in writing this journal, which is not just to be read by me, my levels seem to have been possibly the best they've been in years over this past month. Perhaps, because it is not for a doctor, but rather for research/public display I feel I have to show myself and my sugar levels at their best. So I've been measuring all my food out, eating salads for lunch so that way I don't have to worry about miscalculating carbs and generally keeping on top of it! (Alice: journal)

The journals also allowed participants to get a better sense of their own illness patterns:

I'm generally quite aware of my A. and how it affects my body but since receiving this journal and not knowing what to write about, I've paid a little more attention to my joints. (Aiden: journal)

It has been interesting writing this, though I've changed some of my conclusions over the course of writing it. It feels like I'm always going to be susceptible to feeling low, so I'll have to work with it for the rest of my life, instead of expecting some dramatic moment of complete transformation, I should have known that anyway! Maybe I did. I'm surprised how much my mood flits from one state to another, as I've never 'inventorised' it as such, & how much feeling physically low can get mixed up with being depressed, I know that but it seems really clear looking at a breakdown of it. (Anna: journal)

Entries were fragmented across different topics and across time. This flexibility was important, because illness moments are not constant but are themselves fragmented over daily and weekly routines. Unlike the interview situation, which requires an immediate response, the journals gave participants time to think and remember, to collect their thoughts and feelings, and to depart and return to the task, in their own time. For Ava, keeping a journal began to draw too much attention to her body, and she chose to take a break from journaling, which she then later resumed. Being able to control the pace and nature of data collection, the participants could observe their own lives, providing a record of an ever-changing present, as well as hopes for the future:

Writing this journal has helped me to recognise some of the ways in which I have changed, I don't think I'm deluding myself by seeing them as positive. There are lots of areas for improvement still, I know that! I'd like to feel:

* A lot less anxious
* More confident about my work
* Less threatened by other people
* Less dread
* I'd like to look forward to things instead of thinking catastrophe is around every corner

(Anna: journal)

Together, reflection and spontaneity helped to create a sense of intimacy and participation. More personal, private and secret than any other research medium, the journals became a place within which participants could write about childhood memories, future hopes and sexual relationships. As Ruth Bartlett and Christine Milligan (2015: 9) note, diaries are useful for reporting sensitive or otherwise 'unseen' behaviours, such as sexual activity and sleep. These are experiences that participants might want to share, but feel uncomfortable talking about in person. The act of writing proved less likely to make participants feel self-conscious (with the exception of concerns over correct spelling), and allowed participants to disclose as much, or as little, as they liked. This did not mean that their lives risked becoming overexposed. The project dictated a frame of reference and entries were clearly made with this reference and an audience in mind. As an additional check, when I received each journal I made a point of asking if there was any material which the participant did not want me to include in the study. While I usually made a point of meeting in person to collect the journals, on the one occasion when a journal was returned by post, it was lost in transit.

Video diaries

Eight of the participants chose to make a video diary which they recorded with one of two video cameras, a Sony HDR-SR10E and a Sony HDR-TG7VE, which I had bought for the study with funding from the University of London Central Research Fund. Both video cameras were capable of recording high-quality footage to memory cards, and were small and easy to use. The HDR-SR10E is a typical handycam, while the HDR-TG7VE is an ultra-compact vertical camcorder, which I hoped would be easier for participants to use while performing other activities as it is smaller and lighter to hold. One problem, that I had not anticipated was that it was difficult to rest the HDR-TG7VE on a surface or put it down and continue recording, making hands-free filming impossible. I also bought a lightweight tripod, which one of the participants, who had difficulty moving around with the camera in hand, chose to use. My instructions were informal – I gave the participants basic video camera operating instructions and simply asked them to use the video camera to show and tell about their body and their condition:

> You will have one week with the handycam in which to make a video. It is up to you whether you put yourself in

the frame, but try to think about both the visual and audio components and how you can show and tell about your body and your condition. (Instruction sheet)

In the event, most of the participants recorded their video diaries over longer periods of time than a week, although in many instances filming only took place on a few days, with approximately ten hours of video footage produced in total. Implicit in the instruction sheet was an awareness of the potential for participants to reveal or conceal themselves through the camera, something that we carefully discussed both before filming and after. The visible and audible presence of the participants on screen strongly conflicts with the presumption that good ethical practice requires automatic anonymity for participants (for example, see the British Sociological Association's Statement of Ethical Practice). But as Shamser Sinha and Les Back (2014: 484) argue, this default position 'is an anxious symptom of *ethical hypochondria*, which limits the opportunities to rethink authorship and innovate new formats for research'. Instead of automatically ensuring anonymity and concealing all data that might have revealed the participants' identities, from on-camera shots to voice recordings and filming locations, I decided to work with what Paul Sweetman (2009: 8) has described as an ethics of recognition. I found room for ethical manoeuvre in the Association of American Geographers Statement of Professional Ethics, which states: 'Informants should be asked whether they prefer anonymity or recognition, and the project should be implemented and its results should be presented in keeping with these individuals' preference'. By borrowing this definition I was able to adapt the video diary method as I worked with each participant, so that they controlled the degree to which they revealed their bodies and identities to the video camera. Some participants were comfortable on camera, others preferred not to film themselves directly, and one participant chose to film in silence. In order to maintain her anonymity Anna wrote notes to the video camera, which were then placed as subtitles on the screen. This allowed her to make a video diary without revealing her identity through the recognisable sound of her voice, and ensured her privacy without restricting her participation.

Despite the current popularity of video, the participants in the study were often initially uncomfortable with the idea of filming in public places, being in front of the video camera and recording their own voices. To make recording a video diary less daunting they were encouraged to film short clips of their daily lives. This format meant that long monologues did not dominate the frame, and it allowed everyday sights and sounds to come into focus. The hints and traces of bodies shown in different acts and contexts – at work and at home, exercising, gardening, eating and sleeping – provided glimpses into the participants' lives that would have been hard to access with other methods. Most of the filming took place in the comfort and safety of the participants' homes, but the participants also ventured out with the cameras for walks, to parks, to work, on public transport and to the gym. On one occasion Alice tried to film a hospital appointment, an encounter that challenged her right to film her own body:

> They wouldn't let us film in hospital because I hadn't asked permission, which I find weird because it's all about data protection, and you know that they're allowing CCTV cameras to record you, which is somehow different than when you want to record your own body, but they said if I'd asked permission there wouldn't be a problem, so what can I do – I can do it at home, or like this, outside the hospital. It's strange, the negotiation you have to play with your own body, what can be filmed, what can't be filmed about yourself, purely because you're in a hospital, and who owns your actions or whatever. (Alice: video diary)

The participants also brought their own visual skills to the task of making a video diary, and found their own ways of working with the video camera and their own filmic language. They made different choices about what and how to film, and while cultural references helped them to style their video diaries, they did not appear to influence what was enacted for the video camera. The video diaries ranged from reality television to intimate personal diary, and from action shots to quiet reflections. For example, conducting a *Spendaholics* or *You Are What You Eat* reality television show shock tactic for herself, Alice decided to record a tidy-up of her bedroom on video. She found twenty-two empty Lucozade bottles in her room and lined them up along the foot of her bed. The display quantified the presence of Lucozade in Alice's body and her life and highlighted the significance of this seemingly ordinary drink. Amara used her video diary to discuss her fears in an intimate conversation with her boyfriend. Hidden behind a book, Amara's boyfriend used a camera phone to look back at the video camera while she asked him a series of uncompromisingly honest questions: 'What do you think about my body? Do you think it is unusual? Do you think it is different? How do you feel about the fact that I'm barren?' As Les Back (2004: 137) writes, it would be a mistake to see the lens as only looking one way. During filming, the participants once again became observers of their own lives, and one-way conversations and comments like 'I thought I should show you this' established the presence of an audience who would later see and hear the footage that had been recorded for them, reaffirming the research agenda and the purpose of the diaries.

When filming was completed I transcribed the narratives from the video diaries and integrated them with interview and journal transcripts so that I could analyse the data thematically. By identifying themes across the different methods I was able to support my interpretation of the video diaries with other data and consider them in a broader context. I also wanted to attend to the seemingly mundane and ordinary details of embodied life that were recorded on video. These phenomena often escape talk- and text-based approaches, but were powerfully present in the video diaries. In order to reincorporate these phenomena and the more-than-textual and multisensual elements of the video diaries into my analysis I re-watched the original footage, this time feeling for the less obvious sights and sounds, rather than looking for any underlying or hidden meaning. In what Les Back (2010: 17) describes as a shift 'from being concerned only with "voice" to an attention to soundscape and sound image', I returned to the original footage to listen for the non-verbal noises that had been recorded. Acoustics have their own intimacy and they help us to see differently, working against dominant ways of looking and bringing the viewer into the experience. By 'turning up the background' (Back, 2010: 25) I was able to pick out the bodily noises, for example breathing and footfall, that indicated the presence of bodies that were otherwise imperceptible on screen. Drawing on composer Murray Shafer's seminal book *Tuning the World* (1977), Les Back writes of this kind of listening as a way of taking the soundtrack of the social background seriously:

> The police siren, the children laughing in the street, the jet plane's moan overhead along with the crowing birdsong, the sounds of movement of rubber on tarmac, of internal combustion are invitations to develop a different kind of sociological imagination attentive to the rhythm and aesthetics of life. (Back, 2010: 19)

As he points out, paying attention to these sounds foregrounds the taken-for-granted aspects of everyday life and shows the potential of using sound sociologically, beyond simply recording human voices. Along the same lines, I also 'turned up' the visual background of the video diaries. Watching them back, I began to notice things in the fragments of video – as Eric Laurier (2014: 269) notes, 'Video clips are called "fragments" to remind the viewer that what they are looking at only appears self-contained'. Within the video diaries bodies were perceptible and imperceptible, visible and hidden. Not always shown in their entirety, the traces of bodies were present in other ways. Parts of bodies were shown to camera, shadows were trailed on pavements, and reflections were captured in windows and coffee pots. These visual traces meant that even when the participants' bodies were not directly filmed they remained sensed or felt, and by noticing them I developed a more subtle and nuanced account of embodied everyday life.

Like the journals, the video diaries were not concerned with 'capturing' the real. As Katrina Brown, Rachel Dilley and Keith Marshall write:

> We must start by treating it less in terms of being an objective or factual record of what people do and more as a constructed audio-visual representation that may be used to *evoke* a sense of subjective positions and experiences. (Brown et al, 2008: 2.4)

I have written about the possibilities that video offers for creating a space within which bodies can be seen, heard and felt (Bates, 2013). As Phillip Vannini (2015: 237) writes, 'The evocation of experiences and practices of the human body – in all their non-representational excesses – is precisely where traditional methods, with their excessive emphasis on the discursive or the causative, have left much to be desired'. I suggested that the video camera is beautifully sensate and can be used to record a wide range of bodily sensations, activities and practices, but also pointed out that while video is a useful tool for recording the sensual and affective qualities of bodily experience, these recordings can sometimes be at odds with the embodied sensation they seek to evoke. Anna's footage of running, for example, sends the viewer lurching left and right at a heavy and heaving pace. Although her 'running with camera technique' improved as she went on, the resulting footage contradicts Anna's own experience of running, which helps her manage her depression and makes her feel fluid, light and free. The end result is a dissonance between experience and playback, suggesting that video is much more than a simple or straightforward recording device. The footage documents but it also confounds, it has a life of its own and a relationship with its viewers – as W.J.T. Mitchell (2005) writes, images exert their own power over the living.

Elsewhere, my focus has been less on the materiality of embodiment and more on the emotions, memories and other intangibles that are lived through the body and which saturate the video diaries (Bates, 2015). In the study, video cameras were pointed at heaving asthmatic lungs and aching arthritic shoulders, and they were taken on walks and to the gym, carried on bicycles and held while running. But they were also confided in at night, pointed at loved ones, and taken for walks down memory lane. From action shots to quiet reflections, the range of footage draws attention to the potential of video to incorporate a wide range of sensibilities into the creation of sociological accounts of everyday lives. In her video diary Ava recorded her morning ritual, which includes preparing a glass of water with freshly squeezed lemon. The drink forms part of a complex relationship that Ava has with her rheumatoid arthritis, and the recognition that takes place within the performance of this everyday ritual produces a situation of intimacy. Intimate moments like these reveal the raw and deep power of video footage, as Michael Rich and Jennifer Patashnick write:

> Other forms of data cannot duplicate the audiovisual record of four minutes of a girl coughing, wheezing and gasping for breath as she is increasingly overwhelmed by an asthma exacerbation. (Rich and Patashnick, 2002: 249)

I have shown clips of the video diaries in academic presentations – as Jamie Lorimer (2010: 251) notes, videos 'provide lively materials for subsequent presentation and evocation' - and I have also uploaded two short edited videos to Vimeo, a community for storing and distributing video content online, to accompany a printed article (Bates, 2013). At the same time, I have been cautious not to let the video diaries go public in their entirety or without written companionship. While video offers untapped possibilities for reaching a much wider audience, the video diary footage was not made for this purpose, and just as interview transcripts should not be left to 'speak for themselves' (Back, 2007), the video diaries need to be situated in sociological analysis and interpretation. In fact, the work of editing and sequencing video footage can be seen as paralleling the more standard academic task of selecting and framing quotes from discursive sources when writing up research. Textual and visual data present similar difficulties, and 'it is as easy to select a particular quotation that supports the point one is making as it is to manipulate the framing, lighting or tone of a photograph to present the desired effect' (Knowles and Sweetman, 2004: 13).

There is no companion website or DVD to this book, but stills from the video diaries are included between the pages. As Eric Laurier (2014: 262) notes, 'The problem with stills from videos is that they tend to lose the timing and flow of the visible actions'. These static images lack the motion of video; they are fragments, or snapshots, ripped out of longer sequences. But accompanied by quotations and thick descriptions, they aim to take readers closer to the lives they are reading about, and bring the study to life in colour.

Taking part

While conversations about taking part in the study were ongoing throughout the year in which I conducted my fieldwork, the opportunity to return to the lives of the participants seven years later also presented a chance to talk again, retrospectively, about the experience of being a research participant. This section of the appendix tells about that experience, in the participants' own words. Reflecting on the ups and downs of taking part, the participants highlight the embarrassments and difficulties, as well as the rewards, of being in the study.

> 'One thing that occurred to me, which I've learnt, is that in the process of keeping the diary and doing the video, for me, and for a lot of people who've experienced depression, writing about it, thinking about it, wasn't particularly a good thing for me. Actually I'm better off not thinking about it too much. It just struck me, I felt quite a bit worse doing it. I know rumination is not a good thing for someone like me. I don't know if anyone else experienced that … In many ways, it was a really unhappy time for me. That's one of the complexities of looking back. Maybe it was useful for me to realise that I'm better off not ruminating about my situation, although I may have a natural inclination to do it … But it was very interesting to take part, it made me realise the body is something our culture doesn't necessarily place the right kind of value on. I certainly like my own body much more than I used to. As I get older I sometimes look back and think god, how could I not just treasure the fact that I had a fully functioning body! So that's interesting, but it's just getting older.' (Anna: follow-up interview)

'I think it's super interesting, but I have a confession which is when you sent me the work and the DVD I did not read or watch anything because I didn't want to look at it. It's very difficult for me to hear my own voice. I felt like I trust you; I have been honest, I haven't said anything that I regret. But I don't really know your interpretation of it at this point. Maybe someday I will have enough courage to look.' (Ava: follow-up interview)

'I don't mind taking about myself, it's good to get stuff off your chest, it was quite therapeutic that I could do that. I tried to watch the video but I couldn't watch it, and I haven't let anyone else watch it or read it. I felt a bit embarrassed about that. With the separation, I was ok with it, but if it's someone that knows me, you're not allowed. Not even my wife's read it, not that I would stop her now, but at the time … I think seeing you again this time, it's been quite good for me to have some positive thoughts about it. Because I never stop and think, it's going well, and I should really. We always think about the 5% of crap that's going on rather than the 95%, we should celebrate the good stuff.' (Aiden: follow-up interview)

'I'm always happy to wear my heart on my sleeve. I like talking about myself. I found it interesting when you sent me back the transcript from the interview, I dug it up, I think more than anything my reflections where haven't my kids grown up, but in terms of aches and pains nothing much has really changed.' (Adrian: follow-up interview)

'It was the first time that someone had asked me to think about and verbalise or pour out my experience, and the way that I had been processing the medicalised understanding of my body had been very much an internal process, or getting information from the outside and processing it inside my head, and not really having to expand on it other than to explain to new doctors or boyfriends. And that's why I feel I maybe wasn't the best subject for you, because I didn't really have the words or expression to fully, I didn't have anything formed, it was very much the first time, it felt very public even though it was very private … It was an experience in letting go but also articulating something that I had only really in the modality of experience. And I think that was a really good experience for me, to be a part of your project. It made me think about myself in a different way. I have actually, funnily enough, taken up the journaling element of your project, that has stuck with me, not necessarily throughout but I bring it back when I want to understand what my body is doing with regard to different kinds of medicalised options that have been changing in the past five years. After a long enough time, I get some sense of how the body has changed or how its responding to a different regime.' (Amara: follow-up interview)

'One of the best things I ever did, honestly. When your email came through, I remember it coming through, I was on my bed and having a complete breakdown with the diabetes, just one of those, it's officially called diabetes burnout, who knew, there's a phrase for it. And it was like oh I need to get a grip of it and I just wish there was a place to talk about it, and lo and behold your email came through. I said wow this is obviously what I should do. But it did allow me to vocalise it and make it visible to somebody who wasn't a doctor and actually it allowed me to then experiment with that and to take that further and then with everything else that's gone on with it, honestly yes it was a significant moment to be able to talk to somebody else separate to that world about it, because I think the work is also really important so it was interesting hearing what you were doing.' (Alice: follow-up interview)

Bibliography

Abrahamsson, S. (2014) 'Cooking, eating and digesting: Notes on the emergent normativities of food and speeds', *Time and Society*, 23(3): 287–308.

Améry, J. (1994) *On Aging: Revolt and Resignation*, Bloomington, Indiana University Press.

Back, L. (2004) 'Listening with our eyes: Portraits as urban encounter', in Knowles, C. and Sweetman, P. (Eds) *Picturing the Social Landscape: Visual Methods and the Sociological Imagination*, London, Routledge.

Back, L. (2007) *The Art of Listening*, Oxford, Berg.

Back, L. (2010) Broken devices and new opportunities: Re-imagining the tools of qualitative research. NCRM Working Paper. Available from http://eprints.ncrm.ac.uk/1579/1/0810_broken_devices_Back.pdf

Back, L. (2013) 'Live sociology: Social research and its futures', in Back, L. and Puwar, N. (Eds) *Live Methods*, Oxford, Wiley-Blackwell.

Back, L. (2015) 'Why everyday life matters: Class, community and making life livable', *Sociology*, 49(5): 820–836.

Back, L. and Keith, M. (2014) 'Reflections: Writing cities', in Jones, H. and Jackson, E. (Eds) *Stories of Cosmopolitan Belonging: Emotion and Location*, London, Routledge.

Bartlett, R. and Milligan, C. (2015) *What is Diary Method?*, London, Bloomsbury.

Bates, C. (2013) 'Video diaries: Audio-visual research methods and the elusive body', *Visual Studies*, 28(1): 29–37.

Bates, C. (2015) 'Intimate encounters: Making video diaries about embodied everyday life', in Bates, C. (Ed) *Video Methods: Social Science Research in Motion*, London, Routledge.

Brown, K., Dilley, R. and Marshall, K. (2008) 'Using a head-mounted video camera to understand social worlds and experiences', *Sociological Research Online*, 13(6): 1.

Brownlie, J. and Anderson, S. (2017) 'Thinking sociologically about kindness: Puncturing the blasé in the ordinary city', *Sociology*, 51(6): 1222–1238.

Carel, H. (2008) *Illness: The Cry of the Flesh*, Stocksfield, Acumen.

Carel, H. (2013) 'Bodily doubt', *Journal of Consciousness Studies*, 20(7–8): 178–197.

Ciardi, J. (2013) *The Inferno*, by Dante Alighieri translated by John Ciardi, New York, Signet Classics.

Clifford, J. (1986) 'Introduction: Partial truths', in Clifford, J. and Geertz, M. (Eds) *Writing Culture: The Poetics and Politics of Ethnography*, Berkeley, University of California Press.

Crary, J. (2014) *24/7: Late Capitalism and the Ends of Sleep*, London, Verso.

Department of Health (2012) *Long Term Conditions Compendium of Information*. Available from www.dh.gov.uk/publications

Fraser, M. and Greco, M. (Eds) (2005) *The Body: A Reader*, London, Routledge.

Fuller, M. (2018) *How to Sleep: The Art, Biology and Culture of Unconsciousness*, London, Bloomsbury.

Goffman, E. (1963) *Stigma: Notes on the Management of Spoiled Identity*, Englewood Cliffs, NJ, Prentice Hall.

Hall, T. (2017) *Footwork: Urban Outreach and Hidden Lives*, London, Pluto Press.

Hockey, J., Dilley, R., Robinson, V. and Sherlock, A. (2014) 'The temporal landscape of shoes: A life course perspective', *The Sociological Review*, 62(2): 255–275.

Knowles, C. and Sweetman, P. (Eds) (2004) *Picturing the Social Landscape: Visual Methods and the Sociological Imagination*, London, Routledge.

Kusenbach, M. (2003) 'Street phenomenology: The go-along as ethnographic research tool', *Ethnography*, 4(3): 455-485.

Laurier, E. (2014) 'Noticing', in Lee, R., Castree, N., Kitchin, R., Lawson, V., Paasi, A., Philo, C., Radcliffe, S., Roberts, S. and Withers, C. (Eds) *The SAGE Handbook of Human Geography*, London, Sage.

Lefebvre, H. (2014) *Rhythmanalysis: Space, Time and Everyday Life*, London, Bloomsbury.

Lefebvre, H. and Régulier, C. (2014) 'The rhythmanalytical project', in Lefebvre, H. *Rhythmanalysis: Space, Time and Everyday Life*, London, Bloomsbury.

Lorimer, J. (2010) 'Moving image methodologies for more-than-human geographies', *Cultural Geographies*, 17(2): 237–258.

Louv, R. (2010) *Last Child in the Woods: Saving Our Children from Nature-Deficit Disorder*, London, Atlantic Books.

Mitchell, W.J.T. (2005) *What Do Pictures Want? The Lives and Loves of Images*, Chicago, University of Chicago Press.

Mol, A. (2008) *The Logic of Care: Health and the Problem of Patient Choice*, Abingdon, Routledge.

Perec, G. (2008) *Species of Spaces and Other Pieces*, London, Penguin Classics.

Rice, T. (2008) '"Beautiful murmurs": Stethoscopic listening and acoustic objectification', *The Senses and Society*, 3(3): 293-306.

Rich, M. and Patashnick, J. (2002) 'Narrative research with audiovisual data: Video Intervention/Prevention Assessment (VIA) and NVivo', *International Journal of Social Research Methodology*, 5(3): 245–261.

Sinha, S. and Back, L. (2014) 'Making methods sociable: Dialogue, ethics and authorship in qualitative research', *Qualitative Research*, 14(4): 473–487.

Stoller, P. (1997) *Sensuous Scholarship*, Philadelphia, University of Pennsylvania Press.

Sweetman, P. (2009) 'Just anybody? Images, ethics and recognition', in Leino, R. (Ed) *Just Anybody*, Winchester: The Winchester Gallery/ Winchester School of Art.

Vannini, P. (2015) 'Afterword: Video methods beyond representation: Experimenting with multimodal, sensuous, affective intensities in the 21st century', in Bates, C. (Ed) *Video Methods: Social Science Research in Motion*, London, Routledge.

Vogel, E. and Mol, A. (2014) 'Enjoy your food: On losing weight and taking pleasure', *Sociology of Health and Illness*, 36(2): 305–317.

Williams, S. (2005) *Sleep and Society: Sociological Ventures into the (Un) Known...*, London, Routledge.

Wright Mills, C. (1959) *The Sociological Imagination*, Oxford, Oxford University Press.

Index

A

Abrahamsson, Sebastian 84
acceptance 20, 24, 31, 32, 69, 79, 82, 87, 88
Adam 15, 47, 73
adoption 32, 51, 55
Adrian 16, 27, 41-42, 46, 65-67, 68-69, 76, 88, 96, 105
Aiden 5, 14-15, 16, 25-27, 30-32, 39-40, 43, 65, 75, 77, 82, 83, 85, 88, 90, 97, 105
alcohol 8, 9, 12, 13, 14, 17
Alec 12-13, 23, 27, 32-33
Alice 16-19, 28, 29-30, 37-39, 47-48, 50, 58-60, 67-68, 75, 78, 83, 84, 89, 96, 100, 106
Amara 27-28, 50-52, 53-55, 77, 100, 105-106
Amelia 13-14, 36-37, 76, 96
Améry, Jean 92
Ami 5, 14-15, 45-46, 49, 77
Anna 4, 5-6, 12, 13, 21-23, 27, 35-36, 49, 57-58, 71-72, 75, 77, 78-79, 83, 84, 97, 99, 102, 104
anonymity 3, 99
Anya 5, 11-12, 13, 24, 27, 47, 49, 60-64, 77, 84, 85-86, 89, 92
April 14, 40-41, 46, 52-53, 89
asthma 5, 14, 45-46, 49, 103
Ava 4, 7-11, 12, 13, 16, 19-20, 24-25, 27, 39, 43, 45, 48, 58, 73-75, 82, 83, 84, 87, 88, 90, 96, 97, 103, 105

B

Back, Les 2, 3, 6, 81, 93, 99, 100, 101, 103
Bartlett, Ruth 94, 95, 98
belonging 91-92

bipolar disorder 12, 32
bodily doubt 1, 81, 92
breathing 45, 58, 79, 101
Brown, Katrina 102
Brownlie, Julie 90-91
bruises 28, 46, 48, 58-59, 71
bus 50, 63, 75, 89, 94

C

cane 5, 24, 57, 61, 63, 67
see also walking stick
care 86-88
Carel, Havi 1, 92
children 16, 43, 52, 54-55, 67, 69, 89
Ciardi, John 3
Clifford, James 3, 6
clothing 1, 59
cooking 9, 13, 20, 84
Crary, Jonathan 82-83, 85
cycling 4, 21, 23, 65-66, 103

D

Department of Health 81
depression 4, 5, 12, 13-14, 16, 35-36, 50, 58, 71-72, 76, 78, 102, 104
diabetes 15, 16-17, 28, 29, 47, 59, 67-68, 73, 78, 106
diagnosis 16, 40, 68-69, 95
digestion 8, 12, 84
doctor 2, 8, 26, 27, 40, 49, 53, 69, 77, 96, 105, 106
drawings 2, 77, 93, 94, 95
dream 36, 37, 40

E

epilepsy 40-41, 53

F

family 9, 17, 32-33, 62, 74, 78, 95
fibromyalgia 68
fragments 3, 74, 102, 104
Fraser, Mariam 1-2, 88
Fuller, Matthew 83

G

gardening 77, 78, 79, 100
Goffman, Erving 88-90
guilt 13, 16

H

Hall, Tom 3, 6
Hockey, Jenny 88
holiday 33, 40, 42, 94
hormone replacement therapy (HRT)
    28, 51, 53-54, 77
hospital 2, 40, 51, 61, 100
hypo 17-18, 29-30, 37-39, 83

I

injecting 50, 59-60, 73
insomnia 35-36, 83
insulin pump 67-68
intersex 27, 52-53
intimacy 2, 10, 98, 101, 103
in/visibility 88-91

J

joint hypermobility syndrome 41, 46,
    68
journals 94-98

K

kickboxing 26, 30
kindness 61, 90-91
Knowles, Caroline 103
Kusenbach, Margarethe 95

L

Laurier, Eric 102, 104
Lefebvre, Henri 81, 85
listening 3, 7, 12, 19, 27, 46, 54, 74,
    75, 76, 85, 101
Lorimer, Jamie 103
Louv, Richard 83-84

M

medication 4, 12, 13, 18, 19, 21, 23,
    24, 32, 45, 46, 52-53, 71, 94
mind/body 5-6, 13, 22, 24, 29, 36, 37,
    54, 71-72, 74-76
Mitchell, W.J.T. 102
Mol, Annemarie 86
mood 4, 12-13, 21, 23, 36, 39, 78, 97
muscular dystrophy 5, 11, 24, 47, 60

P

pain 4, 5, 16, 26, 27, 39-40, 41-42, 45,
    58, 65-66, 68-69, 71, 74, 75, 76,
    81, 85, 88, 94, 105
pancreas 16, 47-48, 52, 60, 68
Perec, Georges 95
physiotherapist 24
Polaroids 61, 74
psoriasis 77
psychiatrist 13
public 2, 50, 59, 64-65, 67, 81, 82, 89-
    90, 93, 96, 99, 100, 103, 105

R

rheumatoid arthritis 4, 5, 7-9, 11, 16,
    19, 24-25, 26-27, 30-32, 48, 58, 65,
    73-75, 90, 103
rheumatologist 32, 48, 77
rhythm 81-86
Rice, Tom 3
Rich, Michael 103
routine 1, 4, 7, 9-10, 12, 13, 15, 17,
    19, 21, 27, 32-33, 35, 42, 45, 66,
    68, 73, 78, 79, 82, 85, 87, 90, 95,
    97
running 4, 21-23, 27, 69, 79, 84, 102,
    103

S

scar 51
seizure 14, 40-41, 46, 52-53, 89
sex 13, 16, 29, 98
shoes 5, 23, 57, 58, 66-67, 79, 88
Sinha, Shamser 99
skin 47, 51, 53, 59, 67-68, 73, 74, 77
snapshots 6, 104
society 40, 49-50, 51, 64, 81, 83, 85,
    89
stairs 24, 63-64
stigma 1, 49, 81, 88-90
Stoller, Paul 93

Sweetman, Paul 99
swimming 23, 24, 26, 27, 28, 65, 77

T

taking part 104-106
therapist 36, 78
train 65-66, 94
translation 3
trees 22, 72, 77, 83
trust 24, 37, 41, 71, 79, 105
tube 27, 65, 66, 75, 94

U

Up documentary series 6

V

Vannini, Phillip 102
video diaries 98-104
Vogel, Else 87-88

W

walking 13, 24, 25, 51, 54, 58, 66, 67,
    75, 77, 78, 79, 88
walking stick 89
wheelchair 24, 45, 62
Williams, Simon 83
Wright Mills, C. 93

Y

yoga 9-10, 23, 24, 25, 54, 78